Fatherhood in Midwifery and Neonatal Practice

Note

*Healthcare practice and knowledge are constantly changing and developing
as new research and treatments, changes in procedures, drugs and equipment
become available.*

*The editors and publishers have, as far as is possible, taken care to confirm that the
information complies with the latest standards of practice and legislation.*

Fatherhood in Midwifery and Neonatal Practice

by

Kevin Hugill and Merryl Harvey

QUAY
BOOKS

A division of MA Healthcare Ltd

Quay Books Division, MA Healthcare Ltd, St Jude's Church, Dulwich Road, London
SE24 0PB

British Library Cataloguing-in-Publication Data
A catalogue record is available for this book

ISBN-10: 1-85642-430-8
ISBN-13: 978-1-85642-430-1

Edited by Jessica Anderson

Cover design by Bexi Harris, Fonthill Creative

Publishing Manager: Andy Escott

Printed by Mimeo, Huntingdon, Cambridgeshire

iv

Contents

Foreword

Becoming a father is a major life event, leading to a new aspect of individual identity, and new roles and responsibilities. It is a job for life. The transition to parenthood and becoming 'a father' presents a window of opportunity for support and intervention where health professionals have a positive role to play. This book is aimed at midwives and those working in neonatal care in the course of training and in practice. There is no absolutely right way of providing help and support, but understanding the practical and emotional needs of parents, particularly fathers, and helping them to find their own way and a new equilibrium in what for many is new territory, is now recognised as integral in engaging couples and parents and in supporting families.

The psychological, social and practical issues associated with fatherhood are multiple and the construct itself is many faceted. When does being a father begin? Is it when planning a pregnancy, seeing the results of a pregnancy test, seeing the changes in one's partner, seeing the ultrasound images of the baby, or being present for labour and birth? Adjustment and readjustment take place over time and while the first scans often bring home the reality of a developing baby, they do not necessarily invoke the reality of becoming a 'father'. 'Being there' for many fathers is critical, but we need to be aware of attitudinal and cultural differences that have to be taken into account when working with families.

For some the connection and change in self-image and identity occurs much later, when they hold their new baby and their baby looks at them (Nugent et al, 2007; Brazelton and Nugent, 2011). The power and excitement of meeting the new baby for the first time in this one-to-one way is profound for many fathers and is something that is looked back on with enjoyment and pride.

It is important that established health professionals working in the perinatal field and those in training are able to 'put themselves in the shoes' of fathers and their partners and to see things from a different perspective. This book will enable those working in these specialities to appreciate the context of modern fatherhood, the emotional responses and impact it brings, and the individual differences that are part and parcel not only of responding to such a life-changing event but also adapting to a family life that has become more complicated.

In interacting with parents it is really important always to hold in mind whose baby it is. While in the past fathers were commonly relegated to the corridor, waiting area or corner of the delivery room and expected to just accompany mothers to the neonatal unit, it is now recognised that for the wellbeing and future of mothers, babies and fathers, a positive inclusive approach needs to be taken (Ramchandani et al, 2005; Royal College of Midwives, 2012a, b). Health professionals have an active role to play in responding to the needs of both parents, in information-giving, building confidence and reflecting back to fathers' and mothers' positive images of themselves and their role as parents. Where families are vulnerable, disadvantaged, or the baby is sick, staff need to manage their assumptions, adjust their responses and expectations, and respond to individual needs and circumstances.

The writers of this book are highly experienced and empathic health professionals, who are also researchers, with studies that have involved listening and talking to fathers directly. This involvement is what led to recognising and responding to the need for the present volume in which fathers are seen from a 360 degree perspective. Valuing fathers and their role underpins the whole approach taken, and, supported by both evidence and theory, this book will inform both established practitioners and those in training in an insightful way that can only lead to better and more family-centred practice and care (Staniszewska et al, 2012).

Maggie Redshaw
Senior Research Fellow, Developmental and Health Psychologist
National Perinatal Epidemiology Unit, University of Oxford

References

Brazelton B, Nugent JK (2011) *The Neonatal Behavioral Assessment Scale* (4th edn). MacKeith Press, London

Nugent K, Keefer CH, Minear S, Johnson LC, Blanchard PT (2007) *Understanding newborn behavior and early relationships: The Newborn Behavioral Observations (NBO) system handbook*. Brookes, Baltimore MD

Ramchandani P, Stein A, Evans J, O'Connor TG and the ALSPAC study team (2005) Paternal depression in the postnatal period and child development: A prospective population study. *The Lancet* **365**: 2201–5

Royal College of Midwives (2012a) *Reaching out: Involving fathers in maternity care*. Royal College of Midwives, London

Royal College of Midwives (2012b) *Top tips for involving fathers in maternity care*. Royal College of Midwives, London

Staniszewska S, Brett J, Redshaw M, Hamilton K, Newburn M, Jones N, Taylor L (2012) The POPPY study: Developing a model of family-centred care for neonatal units. *Worldviews on Evidence-Based Nursing*, in press. doi: 10.1111/j.1741-6787.2012.00253.x

Chapter 1

Introducing fathers and fatherhood

Kevin Hugill and Merryl Harvey

Introduction

This book considers fatherhood, an issue of considerable relevance to midwives and neonatal nurses and yet one that has been, to date, largely ignored. The inspiration for this book arose out of our prolonged and extensive contact with fathers in many areas, including care delivery, service management, education and research. We believe that a father's contributions, needs, expectations and wishes should be acknowledged and embraced and that they deserve a higher profile within midwifery and neonatal practice. We seek to arrive at an appreciation of fatherhood and what fathers themselves experience during pregnancy, childbirth and the early postnatal period.

In this book, we aim to link theory, research and practice together in an informative and authoritative, yet accessible and relevant way. Of particular note and relevance to this endeavour is our use of summary key points and case histories based upon real-life events together with reflective questions and exercises within each chapter. These serve to support readers in integrating the material in each chapter into their everyday experiences and practice. In so doing, we challenge some of the prevailing beliefs, myths, understandings and ideas about fathers and fatherhood, particularly in relation to midwifery and neonatal practice.

The roles of fathers in families, and men and women's expectations of fatherhood, have undergone considerable change in recent years (O'Brien, 2005; Brannen and Nilsen, 2006; Equal Opportunities Commission, 2006; 2007). Fathers in midwifery and neonatal care environments can offer a unique perspective into these changes and how they inform and shape midwifery and neonatal practice. Steen et al (2011) carried out a metasynthesis of 23 international English language qualitative research papers concerning fathers' experiences of maternity care. They concluded that when fathers seek to engage with maternity care services and healthcare professionals they are viewed as neither patient nor visitor. Consequently, fathers remain somewhat isolated and seemingly inhabit an undefined emotional and physical space between that of unencumbered visitor and engaged participant. This indeterminate identity is a source of much angst for fathers and healthcare professionals alike and may help explain the source of fathers' reported marginalisation, exclusion and dissatisfaction. Much study relating to men's roles and expectations around pregnancy, birth and childcare has continued to view men as peripheral and supporters of mothers (Draper, 2002a, b; Finnbogadóttir et al, 2003) rather than as equal participants. However, despite men's relative invisibility, expectant fathers exert considerable influence over their partner's choice of birth place (Bedwell et al, 2011) and baby feeding decisions (Pontes et al, 2008; Sweet and Darbyshire, 2009).

In more general terms, the focus on fathers and fatherhood is becoming stronger (Friedewald et al, 2005). Fatherhood is an increasingly topical subject for the media, researchers, user groups and policy makers (Department of Health, Department for Education and Skills, 2004; Mander, 2004; Burgess, 2006; World Health Organization, 2007). This attention is in sharp contrast to the recent past when parenting research focused almost exclusively on mothers and, as a consequence, fathers have, to date, been under-represented in the parenting literature (Lewis and O'Brien, 1987; Burghes et al, 1997; Pruett, 1998; Barclay and Lupton, 1999; Macfadyen et al, 2011). When conducting a literature search, it soon becomes apparent that many research studies appearing to investigate 'parenting' issues do not, on closer scrutiny, include fathers (Condon and Corkindale, 1998; Levy-Shiff et al, 1998; Hess et al, 2004). Studies that do involve fathers often only include a small number in comparison to the number of mothers. Indeed Pruett (1998) makes the interesting but unsubstantiated suggestion that, in the context of research and other related literature, the word 'parent' means 'mother' 75% of the time.

There are a number of possible reasons for this under-representation of fathers. Until the recent past, limited information was documented about a child's father, particularly if the parents were not married. Even if the details were known, fathers were usually less accessible to researchers (Jackson, 1983; Lewis and O'Brien, 1987; Macfadyen et al, 2011), primarily because maternity and early childhood services were almost exclusively mother-focused. Patterns of work in paid employment might also have meant that some fathers were difficult to access. It is also probably the case that fathers were deemed less important than mothers in relation to a child's wellbeing or indeed, that fathers did not have needs or experiences that were worth investigating. As a consequence any father involved in parenting research in the past tended to be recruited via the mother, almost as an afterthought. In the past few years, the balance has begun to shift and the significance of fathers is gradually being recognised, particularly in relation to the perinatal period and a child's long-term wellbeing, albeit that the current focus on fathers is often presented as pathologising them in terms of the detrimental impact of the absent or uninvolved father (Jackson, 1983; Westwood, 1996; Burghes et al, 1997; Sullivan-Lyons, 1998; Torr, 2003; Mander, 2004).

Why are fathers important?

The involvement of fathers in the lives of their children has long-term social and economic benefit not only for the fathers themselves but also for their children, their partners and society in general (Burghes et al, 1997; Beardshaw, 2001; Friedewald et al, 2005; Allen et al, 2007; World Health Organization, 2007). More specifically, it is often argued that a father's involvement promotes not only a child's physical and emotional wellbeing and social development, which in turn, is associated with a reduced incidence of criminality, antisocial behaviour and substance abuse; but also a child's better educational achievement; improved interaction and empathy with others; and higher levels of self-esteem (Vandenberg, 2000; Lewis and Warin, 2001; Allen et al, 2007; Schoppe-Sullivan et al, 2008; Department of Health, 2010). However, it should be noted that not all of the literature making these claims provides statistical evidence to substantiate a correlation between the involvement of a child's father and these factors.

One way of determining the impact of father involvement is to compare children of fathers with and without depression; the assumption being that fathers with depression would be less directly involved in the lives of their children. In a population study of childhood, paternal depression was found to influence a child's behaviour; boys aged 3.5 years of fathers with depression showed more conduct and hyperactivity problems than boys of fathers without depression (Ramchandani et al, 2005). However, the assumption that paternal depression equates with less involvement may not be correct. It should also be noted that the study found gender differences whereby changes in the behaviour of girls were less apparent. It can therefore be seen just from this example, that the impact of father involvement is multifaceted and much more complex than it may initially seem. The intricacies of a father's involvement in the perinatal period will be explored in more detail in the following chapters.

The drive to engage fathers

An increasing number of initiatives in the UK over recent years illustrate the drive to include fathers more readily in the lives of their children. Pregnancy, childbirth and early parenthood have been recognised as being appropriate time-points to capture a father's involvement. Fathers who are involved during pregnancy are more likely to maintain their involvement after the birth (Burgess, 2008). With the increasing absence of the extended family, fathers are also usually the main source of support for mothers during the perinatal period. This therefore provides an ideal opportunity to engage and involve them (Pruett, 1998; McVeigh et al, 2002; Chief Nursing Officers of England, Northern Ireland, Scotland and Wales, 2011).

Whilst the focus of many recent initiatives is on the more general provision of maternity and early childhood services, they also include strategies to engage and involve fathers. For example, the National Service Framework (NSF) for Children, Young People and Maternity Services emphasises the need for greater involvement of fathers at all stages of a child's life (Department of Health, Department for Education and Skills, 2004). Suggestions about the ways in which this could be done include ensuring birth environments are welcoming to fathers and the provision of support for fathers when problems develop during pregnancy and/or when a newborn baby is ill (Department of Health, Department for Education and Skills, 2004). Other examples of initiatives include the National Institute for Health and Clinical Excellence (NICE) guidelines for postnatal care which identify the need to enable both mothers and fathers to nurture their baby (NICE, 2006), and the Royal College of Midwives' (2012) *Reaching out: Involving fathers in maternity care*, which identifies strategies to involve fathers from pregnancy to fatherhood.

A range of other initiatives over the past decade has emphasised the need to engage and involve fathers (Department of Health, 2007, 2010; Department for Children, Schools and Families, Department of Health 2009; Chief Nursing Officers of England, Northern Ireland, Scotland and Wales, 2011). Probably one of the most important of these was the 'Sure Start' scheme which was set up to combat social exclusion, address problems associated with child poverty and to promote parental involvement (National Audit Office, 2006). By 2010, 3500 Sure Start Centres were supporting and empowering families in the UK (Department of Health, 2010). As the drive to involve fathers has gathered momentum, at least a passing reference to the father has now become evident in almost every initiative or directive relating to pregnancy, childbirth or early parenthood. However, whilst the intent may be apparent, the extent to which these proposed initiatives and strategies have been implemented or had any impact on service delivery, healthcare professional attitudes and practice, or individual families is unclear.

These initiatives are not just one-sided attempts to require service providers or individual healthcare professionals to involve fathers more readily, many also emphasise the importance of fathers acknowledging their responsibilities; an approach that many fathers would embrace (Fatherhood Institute, 2008).

However, other fathers may view this as a step too far and regard some of the strategies outlining their responsibilities as being retaliatory. For example, the Child Support Act 1991 highlights the financial responsibilities of fathers, and the Criminal Justice Act 1991 outlines the accountability of both parents for a child's behaviour (Burghes et al, 1997). The current drive to increase the number of fathers documenting their name on their child's birth registration (Department for Work and Pensions, 2008) may also be regarded by some fathers as being punitive. Whilst the Fatherhood Institute (2008) attests that most fathers welcome this move, it could be argued that this organisation might not be representative of all fathers.

It is not just Government directives that have highlighted the importance of fathers. User groups have also taken the opportunity to drive forward recognition of the need to facilitate paternal involvement and they have given particular attention to the provision of maternity and neonatal services (Fatherhood Institute, 2008; Bliss, 2009). Recommendations include the provision of facilities enabling fathers to stay with their partner after the birth, more inclusive parentcraft classes and the adoption of a truly family-centred philosophy of care (Fatherhood Institute, 2008; Bliss, 2009). However, some of these suggestions have stimulated debate, particularly among midwives (Fisher, 2008; Fyle, 2008), some of whom feel proposed strategies could compromise care and in some instances put mothers and babies at risk (Fyle, 2008). It would appear, therefore, that there is sometimes dissonance between the perceived needs of fathers and those who are responsible for service delivery. Despite this contention, the drive to involve fathers more readily is evident.

Over time the roles and responsibilities of fathers have fluctuated. During the past few decades, the balance has changed again and fathers now usually play a more active role in the lives of their children than did their own father or grandfathers. The increased involvement of fathers is particularly evident in relation to childbirth whereby their presence and participation in their partner's care is now usually expected (Burghes et al, 1997; Shulman and Seiffge-Krenke, 1997). Many men are also now involved in the care of their children (Macfadyen et al, 2011) and an increasing number are their child's primary carer (Beardshaw, 2001). This increased involvement has become regarded as being the 'gold standard' or an essential feature of the 'new' father. Research, government policy and the mainstream media have given aspects of 'good' and 'bad' fathering much attention in recent years, with a strong emphasis on the negative effect of absent or negligent fathers (Jackson, 1983; Burghes et al, 1997; Sullivan-Lyons, 1998; Torr, 2003; Mander, 2004). However, classification of fathers in this way has been criticised as being too polarising because the majority of fathers adopt the middle ground (Lewis and Warin, 2001). Whilst most men would welcome opportunities to be more involved in their child's life (Henwood and Procter, 2003; Torr, 2003; Gregory and Milner, 2011) this can present challenges. The reconfiguration of families, and cultural, work and financial pressures mean that some men are less involved in their child's life than they would like to be.

The decline of effective fatherhood role models in society has also been noted as an influential factor for both men and women in determining their view of fatherhood (Condon et al, 2004). Perception of the father role is usually shaped in a direct way by people's culture, age, experiences, beliefs and the expectations of their family and friends (Peterson, 2008). In addition, a woman's negative experience of being fathered may make her less inclined to encourage the involvement of her child's father. Consequently, whilst the 'new' father may be evident in some families, the more traditional aspects of the father's role may persist in others (Lewis and O'Brien, 1987; Burgess, 1997; Lupton and Barclay, 1997).

Layout of this book

Each of the following chapters explores a particular focus on fatherhood. Key points, case histories and reflective activities are included to encourage readers to reflect upon their own practice and to embed the material in this book into their everyday work. *Chapters 2 and 3* develop the context for much of our subsequent discussion. In *Chapter 2*, fatherhood is defined and key factors that have influenced the way the roles of fathers have changed and evolved over time are explored. *Chapter 3* introduces some of the ideas about men's transitions to fatherhood, how men make emotional connections to their children and bring together their (and others') preconceptions with everyday realities. In this chapter we seek to reconcile everyday realities by considering fatherhood in less favourable circumstances. Two examples illustrate some of the complexities and challenges, specifically in mental illness and depression, and young fatherhood.

The impact of fathers being present during normal and complicated childbirth forms the focus for *Chapter 4*. In this chapter we explore some of the key drivers and strategies to promote greater father involvement in childbirth and look at how these have changed over time. We also explore the experiences of fathers of being present during the resuscitation of their baby at delivery.

Chapter 5 moves beyond the period of birth and looks at fathers in the postnatal period. Continuing our theme of fatherhood in normality and in less common circumstances we consider fathers' experiences in neonatal units in contrast to fatherhood in general. In particular we focus upon the stresses and emotional responses of fathers as they seek to reconcile their prior expectations of fatherhood with the everyday realities that they face.

The final chapter reviews the key themes highlighted within this book. We look to the future both in relation to practice and increasing the involvement of fathers in parenting research. We draw together the research, policy and governance literature and make it relevant to practice. The reflective exercises in this chapter ask readers to consider the effects of their own experiences, values and belief systems on their interactions with fathers before posing the difficult question about whose business it is to support fathers anyway?

References

Allen S, Daly K with Father Involvement Research Alliance (2007) *The effects of father involvement: An updated research summary of the evidence*. Centre for Families, Work and Well-Being, Guelph ON

Barclay L, Lupton D (1999) The experiences of new fatherhood: A socio-cultural analysis. *Journal of Advanced Nursing* **29**(4): 1013–20

Beardshaw T (2001) Supporting the role of fathers around the time of birth. *MIDIRS Midwifery Digest* **11**: 476–9

Bedwell C, Houghton G, Richens Y, Lavender T (2011) 'She can choose, as long as I'm happy with it': A qualitative study of expectant fathers' views on birth place. *Sexual and Reproductive Healthcare* **2**: 71–5

Bliss (2009) *The Bliss Baby Charter Standards*. Bliss, London

Brannen J, Nilsen A (2006) From fatherhood to fathering: Transmission and change among British fathers in four generation families. *Sociology* **40**(2): 335–52

Burgess A (1997) *Fatherhood reclaimed: The making of the modern father*. Vermillion, London

Burgess A (2006) *The costs and benefits of active fatherhood: Evidence and insights to inform the development of policy and practice*. Fathers Direct, London

Burgess A (2008) *Maternal and infant health in the perinatal period: The father's role*. The Fatherhood Institute, Abergavenny

Burghes L, Clarke L, Cronin N (1997) *Fathers and fatherhood in Britain*. Family Policy Studies Centre, London

Chief Nursing Officers of England, Northern Ireland, Scotland and Wales (2011) *Midwifery 2020: Delivering expectations*. Jill Rogers Associates and Department of Health, Cambridge and London

Child Support Act 1991. Available from: http:www.legislation.gov.uk/ukpga/1991/48/c (accessed 25 March 2012)

Condon JT, Boyce P, Corkindale CJ (2004) The first-time fathers study: A prospective study of the mental health and well-being of men during the transition to parenthood. *Australian and New Zealand Journal of Psychiatry* **38**(1): 56–64

Condon JT, Corkindale CJ (1998) The assessment of parent-to-infant attachment: Development of a self-report questionnaire instrument. *Journal of Reproductive and Infant Psychology* **16**: 57–76

Criminal Justice Act 1991. Available from: http:www.legislation.gov.uk/ukpga/1991/53/c (accessed 25 March 2012)

Department for Children, Schools and Families, Department of Health (2009) *Healthy lives, brighter futures*. Department of Health, London

Department of Health (2007) *Maternity Matters: Choice, access and continuity of care in a safe service*. Department of Health, London

Department of Health (2010) *Maternity and early years: Making a good start to family life*. HM Government, London

Department of Health, Department for Education and Skills (2004) *National service framework for children, young people and maternity services – Maternity*. Department of Health, London

Department for Work and Pensions (2008) *Joint birth registration: Recording responsibility*. The Stationery Office, Norwich

Draper J (2002a) 'It's the first scientific evidence': Men's experience of pregnancy confirmation. *Journal of Advanced Nursing* **39**(6): 563–70

Draper J (2002b) 'It was a real good show': The ultrasound scan, fathers and the power of visual knowledge. *Sociology of Health and Illness* **24**(6): 771–95

Equal Opportunities Commission (2006) *Twenty-first century dad*. Equal Opportunities Commission, Manchester

Equal Opportunities Commission (2007) *The state of the modern family*. Equal Opportunities Commission, Manchester

Fatherhood Institute (2008) *The dad deficit: The missing piece of the maternity jigsaw*. Fatherhood Institute, Abergavenny

Finnbogadóttir H, Crang Svalenius E, Persson EK (2003) Expectant first time fathers' experiences of pregnancy. *Midwifery* **19**(2): 96–105

Fisher D (2008) The dad deficit: The missing piece of the maternity jigsaw. *Midwives* **Oct/Nov**: 17

Fyle J (2008) Mid-husband? *Midwives* **Aug/Sept**: 40

Friedewald M, Fletcher R, Fairbairn H (2005) All-male discussion forums for expectant fathers: Evaluation of a model. *Journal of Perinatal Education* **14**(2): 8–18

Gregory A, Milner S (2011) Fathers and work–life balance in France and the UK. *International Journal of Sociology and Social Policy* **31**(1-2): 34–52

Henwood K, Procter J (2003) The 'good father': Reading men's accounts of paternal involvement during the transition to first-time fatherhood. *British Journal of Social Psychology* **42**(3): 337–55

Hess CR, Teti DM, Hussey-Gardner B (2004) Self-efficacy and parenting of high-risk infants: The moderating role of parent knowledge of infant development. *Applied Developmental Psychology* **25**(4): 423–37

Jackson B (1983) *Fatherhood*. George Allen & Unwin, London

Levy-Shiff R, Dimitrovsky L, Shulman S, Har-Even D (1998) Cognitive appraisals, coping strategies and support resources as correlates of parenting and infant development. *Developmental Psychology* **34**: 1417–27

Lewis C, O'Brien M (1987) What good are dads? *Father Facts* **1**: 1–12

Lewis C, Warin J (2001) Constraints on fathers: Research, history and clinical practice. In: Lewis C, O'Brien M (eds) *Reassessing fatherhood*. Sage, London

Lupton D, Barclay L (1997) *Constructing fatherhood*. Sage, London

Macfadyen A, Swallow V, Santacroce S, Lambert H (2011) Involving fathers in research. *Journal for Specialists in Pediatric Nursing* **16**: 216–19

McVeigh CA, Baafi M, Williamson M (2002) Functional status after fatherhood: An Australian study. *Journal of Obstetric, Gynaecologic and Neonatal Nursing* **31**(2): 165–71

Mander R (2004) *Men and maternity*. Routledge, London

National Audit Office (2006) *Sure start children centres*. The Stationery Office, London

National Institute for Health and Clinical Excellence (2006) *Routine postnatal care of women and their babies*. National Institute for Health and Clinical Excellence, London

O'Brien M (2005) *Shared caring: Bringing fathers into the frame. Working Paper Series 18*. Equal Opportunities Commission, Manchester

Peterson SW (2008) Father surrogate: Historical perceptions and perspectives of men in nursing and their relationship with fathers in the NICU. *Neonatal Network* **27**: 239–43

Pontes CM, Alexandrino AC, Osório MM (2008) The participation of fathers in the breastfeeding process: Experiences, knowledge, behaviors and emotions. *Jornal Pediatria (Rio J)* **84**(4): 357–64

Pruett KD (1998) Role of the father. *Pediatrics* **102**: 1253–61

Ramchandani P, Stein A, Evans J, O'Connor TG, and the ALSPAC study team (2005) Paternal depression in the postnatal period and child development: A prospective population study. *The Lancet* **365**: 2201–5

Royal College of Midwives (2012) *Reaching out: Involving fathers in maternity care*. Royal College of Midwives, London

Schoppe-Sullivan SJ, Brown GL, Cannon EA, Mangelsdorf SC, Sokolowski MS (2008) Maternal gatekeeping, coparenting quality and fathering behavior in families with infants. *Journal of Family Psychology* **22**: 389–98

Shulman S, Seiffge-Krenke I (1997) *Fathers and adolescents*. Routledge, London

Steen M, Downe S, Bamford N, Edozien L (2011) Not-patient and not-visitor: A metasynthesis of fathers' encounters with pregnancy, birth and maternity care. *Midwifery* doi:10.1016/j.midw.2011.06.009

Sullivan-Lyons J (1998) Men becoming fathers: 'Sometimes I wonder how I'll cope'. In: Clement S (ed) *Psychological perspectives on pregnancy and childbirth.* Churchill Livingstone, Edinburgh

Sweet L, Darbyshire P (2009) Fathers and breast feeding very-low-birthweight preterm babies. *Midwifery* **25**: 540–53

Torr J (2003) *Is there a father in the house?* Radcliffe Medical Press, Abingdon

Vandenberg KA (2000) Supporting parents in the NICU: Guidelines for promoting parent confidence and competence. *Neonatal Network* **19**(8): 63–4

Westwood S (1996) Feckless fathers: Masculinities and the British state. In: Mac A, Ghaill M (eds) *Understanding masculinities.* Buckingham: Open University Press

World Health Organization (2007) *Fatherhood and health outcomes in Europe.* World Health Organization, Copenhagen

Chapter 2

Fatherhood: Key ideas and influences

Kevin Hugill and Merryl Harvey

Introduction

In many respects fatherhood needs no explanation; everyone seems to have an understanding about who fathers are and what they do, but herein is one of the central problems with studying fatherhood, its ubiquity and unacknowledged entanglement with the everyday. There are many unquestioned assumptions about fatherhood together with numerous and sometimes contradictory explanations of it. No one seems to agree about what modern fatherhood involves and what it means for men themselves, their families and society in general. This chapter sets the scene for much of our subsequent discussion about fatherhood in midwifery and neonatal practice. Biological, sociological, political and psychological perspectives are drawn on to review the wider contemporary understandings of fatherhood. Some key ideas and influences upon fathers and fatherhood are highlighted, emphasising the nature of change in men's lives and the effect of a number of social transformations. The chapter ends with a case history that invites readers to reflect upon their own experiences of being a father or being fathered and how these experiences can relate to practice.

Fathers and fatherhood

Fatherhood describes the wider cultural context within which an individual man's fathering behaviours and experiences take place. Ideas about fatherhood remain comparatively less studied and articulated than do those about motherhood. However, in the past 20 years fatherhood research has seen substantial growth, both in the UK and internationally, partially redressing this imbalance. Ideas about what it means to be a father have over this time become more complex and subtle in their distinctions. Social and cultural assumptions about what it means to be a mother or father have considerable continuity, yet they are not fixed. Over time they have changed, and consequently our understandings of both motherhood and fatherhood continue to evolve and are open to debate. For example, the terminology used in discussions about fathers and fatherhood is broad and subject to many cultural distinctions and ideas about men and women's power relationships. English language colloquial terms to refer to fathers in everyday use include, 'dad', 'dada', 'dar', 'daddy', 'pop', 'pa', 'pater', 'sir', 'boss' and 'old man'. The choice and use of these terms can reveal details about the user's geography, social class and age. Individuals may also use different terms in different contexts and this usage may be a means of conveying a number of messages that may include deference, emotional connection or, conversely, disrespect.

The noun father has many understandings in language, its widest use is to refer to the male parent; an acknowledgement of a man's biological contribution to his children. However, other uses of the word are widely evident and deeply entrenched in our culture and language. In more general terms, the word father is used to denote, amongst others, a male ancestor; any person acting in a paternal capacity; an originator of an idea (like, Freud the father of psychoanalysis or Hippocrates the father of Western medicine); in a spiritual sense, as a title of respect (like, priests or monks); or even in politics to denote the leader or founder of a country. In the context of this book we use the word to denote the male parent. Because of the complexities associated with these linguistic turns and debates and the sometimes problematic use of language, fatherhood research has become highly politicised in some quarters. To acknowledge and emphasise some of these issues, paternity or biological fatherhood is often considered separately from fatherhood as a social phenomenon (Woollett and Nicolson, 1998).

The ways in which individual men relate to their roles as fathers and how others relate to them as fathers are deeply embedded within our culture. Lupton and Barclay (1997) argue that fatherhood is not solely constructed through conscious processes and that other realms of knowledge are evident. They suggest that for individual men and women fatherhood is recalled and viewed through avenues of experience, such as touch, smell and amorphous memories of infancy and early childhood and that these are as influential as wider social processes. Connell (1987) proposed that in addition to widely understood biological interpretations of fatherhood there are five further dimensions of its definition. These he labels, social, cultural, symbolic, political, economic and legal (Connell, 1987). It is likely that differing ideas about the content and relative importance of these various facets of fatherhood lead to diverging meanings and understandings of what fatherhood is and what it involves. Consequently, in order to gain a more complete understanding of what fatherhood means, it is important to consider it within biological, psychological, social, economic, political and personal frames of reference.

The remainder of this chapter begins to consider some of the key influences and how they have shaped and informed fatherhood. Subsequent chapters incorporate these various facets of fatherhood to explore men's experiences of fatherhood in real life, everyday and less usual circumstances. In so doing the hope is to begin to unravel and delineate how fatherhood is defined and lived by men themselves and how it is experienced by their families.

Masculinity and fatherhood

Gender affects individuals across their lives by culturally prescribing or proscribing certain behaviours and choices (Smiler, 2004). Gender identity is developed by expressing behaviour in one way more than another depending upon both self-identity and perception of feminine and masculine traits (Woodhill and Samuels, 2004). Men and women's gender identities (masculinity and femininity) are in the main largely learnt through cultural socialisation in early childhood (Mugai, 1999). Masculinity has important effects upon men's self-identities and gendered aspects of fathering (Vuori, 2009). For example, it is known that fathers have considerable influence on gender role development in both boys and girls (Easterbrooks and Goldberg, 1984). Relatively little is known about how boys are socialised to become future fathers, and what is known about the links between childhood experiences and fatherhood behaviours is often contradictory (Cabrera et al, 2000). Understanding what it means to be a man, the so-called 'meaning of manhood' or 'manliness', varies across different social contexts and historical timescales (Seidler, 1997; Finn and Henwood, 2009). It is important to appreciate that whilst all societies are able to provide accounts of the effects of gender, not all have developed concepts of masculinity as it is understood in industrialised countries (Connell, 1995). Therefore, masculinity has many different possible interpretations and as a consequence remains a somewhat contested concept. This may have implications for healthcare professionals who work across cultural boundaries; in such circumstances there is a need for a more nuanced understanding of whether they and their interventions may be more or less acceptable.

Foyster (1999) traces the historical rise of patriarchal forces with its ideas about male authority and female subordination to political events taking place in Europe in the 17th century. During this time political theorists seeking to justify the monarchy sought to draw parallels between the rights and power of the king over the state and its peoples to the rights and power of the father in the family. In effect, in seeking to justify the king's dominion over the state and its populace, gender roles became fully proscribed and by extension men's dominion over women. Early feminist writers drew attention to the central role of gender in developing our subjectivity. Over the past 30 years dominant, or what are often referred to as hegemonic, forms of masculinity have been particularly challenged by feminist critical assessments of the relationships between men and women. The 1970s witnessed an increase in the study of men as gendered individuals, in part due to these feminist critiques of gender (Smiler, 2004). From this time many male and men's studies researchers have also sought, alongside feminist researchers, to question the taken-for-granted ideas about individual difference and agency contained in notions of stereotypical masculinity (Hearn, 1992; 1996; Connell, 1995; Connell and Messerschmidt, 2005).

In the 1990s, debate about the place and role of fathers in families became a subject of considerable academic, media and political attention. There were two main threads to this debate and these centred on questions about whether families needed fathers and if so what sort of fathers they should be (Collier, 2001). This highly polarised debate has continued to inform contemporary concerns about fathers, viewing them as equal and involved, or pathologising them as uninvolved and absent from the home (Lewis, 2000). This continued framing of fatherhood in negative cultural images and in need of change has emerged, according to Seidler (2007), from a limited focus upon men's power relationships, and is problematic. Connell (2005) adds that ideas about changing men and their behaviours cannot be reduced to questions solely concerned with 'how to change men's behaviours' without some consideration of the power relationships between men and women. Nevertheless, considering one group (men) in isolation betrays questionable assumptions about how to achieve social change and assumes that focusing upon men rather than women, or women and men is the most effective strategy (Collier, 2002).

More recent years have witnessed a shift away from the belief that men's gendered lives can be incorporated into a single theoretical point of view (Finn and Heywood, 2009). Partly in response to these challenges to unified understandings of masculinity, Connell (2005) proposed a relational model of masculinity that sought to address some of the deficiencies in traditional ideas about masculinity. In this he perceives masculinity as sets of gendered relationships between men and women within a larger system of relationships which often involve power interactions. Consequently, he conceptualises masculinity in the plural, as a series of interconnected masculinities, in order to account for the many differing possible sets of relationship (Connell, 2005). This plural view of masculinity is increasingly evident in the literature on men. It is representative of the diversity of men's lives and recognises the complexity, fragmentation and differentiation of traditional ideas about masculinity. In some respects masculinities only exist in contrast to other ideas about masculinity and femininities and are consequently rather difficult to define. In effect, Smiler (2004) suggests that masculinities are a phenomenon that men themselves and other men and women practice, perform and construct. Nevertheless, common aspects of all masculinities, regardless of their origins and points of view, seem to include a defining set of behaviours and characteristics, which relate to a particular and defined hypothetical group of the male sex. As such, all ideas about masculinities are inevitably social constructs that reflect and exist within a gendered, historical and cultural world view (Seidler, 1997; Connell, 2005).

In the past, particularly in Western world views, men were stereotypically considered to be on an emotional and physical level that was detached and alienated from, and with little connectedness to, the domestic world and family life (Hochschild, 1994; Duncombe and Marsden, 1998; 1999). Despite attempts in recent years to rearticulate ideas about masculinity to take into account women's agency, embodiment, geography and the dynamics of gender relationships, such views have continued to inform notions about men and women (Connell and Messerschmidt, 2005). In most Western societies, to varying degrees, both male and female gender traits retain their place as a point of reference in people's subjectivity and embodiment. As such, gender, and its effects upon fathers through masculinity, can be a helpful and important conceptual lens to help us consider fatherhood research.

Despite the advances of feminism in addressing imbalances of power between men and women in society, patriarchy (men's relative power dominance over women) continues to pervade much social interaction (Hearn, 2004). Men remain to some degree both structurally and interpersonally dominant in many spheres of life, although this position does not infer that there are no differences between individual men and their relationships with women. Indeed men, like women, are not a homogenous group; men can and do feel powerless despite apparent privileges conferred by their gender (Collinson and Hearn, 1996; Segal, 1997). For example, many fathers in maternity care find themselves in situations that they have no control over and that they are relatively powerless to influence. Some men may find this situation problematic and difficult to cope with. There is therefore a need for greater appreciation among healthcare professionals of the often unstated variations in individual men's understanding of gendered relationships and how these can affect them as fathers, so that services can be planned to best meet their needs.

Fatherhood in law

In the past 20 years, increasingly sophisticated reproductive technologies have come into widespread use. This means that biological presumptions of fatherhood may no longer always hold. Fatherhood does not exist in people's private lives alone but has additional public and political elements which influence it. Contemporary ideas about and definitions of fatherhood have entered the domain of family legislation. Gaining an understanding of legal perspectives on fatherhood has important implications for practice, particularly in relation to medical consent and decision-making. The laws regarding parenthood generally, and fatherhood in particular, have been continuously evolving over the past two decades. This section examines fatherhood in law from a UK statutory point of view.

Prior to the Family Law Reform Act 1987 only married men automatically had parental responsibility for their children. An unmarried father only acquired legal parenthood if the child's mother agreed to him having his name on the birth register. The Family Law Reform Act 1987 enabled an unmarried father, via a court order, to have his name on the birth register without the consent of the mother. Whilst this conferred fatherhood, it did not automatically bestow parental responsibility; fathers could acquire this via a Parental Responsibility Order. Key aspects of parental responsibility include protecting the child, consenting to treatment and allowing the disclosure of confidential information.

The Children Act 1989 set the precedent by introducing and defining the concept of parental responsibility and stating that the best interests of the child, over and above those of the parents and family, should be the central focus of all actions and decisions regarding a child. This principal has been maintained in all subsequent legislation affecting children. As a consequence of the Child Support Act 1991 the biological father became financially responsible for his child, thus reinforcing the breadwinner responsibilities that have long been associated with fatherhood. Nevertheless, evidence from the Child Support Agency shows that only two-thirds of fathers paid their required maintenance in 2007 (Department for Work and Pensions, 2007). However, in some cases the opposite situation has occurred with some men eventually receiving compensation for paternity fraud, when they had supported a child who, unbeknown to them, was not their biological offspring (Draper, 2007; McVeigh, 2007).

The requirement for unmarried fathers to apply for a Parental Responsibility Order ended with the Adoption and Children Act 2002. This Act automatically gave an unmarried father joint parental responsibility when his name was entered onto the birth register. A father does not lose his parental responsibility if he does not live with his child. The same is true if he separates from or divorces the child's mother. Irrespective of where he lives or his subsequent relationship with the child's mother, a father will retain parental responsibility and should be treated on a par with the mother in all decisions or disputes regarding the child. It is interesting to note that biological fathers became financially responsible for their children 11 years before they automatically acquired parental responsibility. It is this dichotomy that has provoked some fathers to take direct, high profile action to highlight what they regard to be their plight.

There are three other important factors to be considered regarding the legal situation pertaining to fatherhood. The first is when the father is aged 18 years of age or less. Legally, at this age, he is a child himself (Webb, 2008). If he is aged 16 to 18 years he may be able to consent for himself if he is deemed capable, for example, to medical treatment or participation in a research study, but he will be unable to consent for his child. The second factor is fatherhood arising from sperm donation. The consenting male partner of the woman having treatment is legally regarded as being the child's father; his name is entered onto the birth register and he automatically acquires parental responsibility for the child. Finally, when a child is the subject of a care order in favour of a Local Authority, the parents share parental responsibility with the Local Authority.

Negotiating the legal situation regarding fathers can be a potential minefield for healthcare professionals. The area is subject to frequent amendments and reinterpretations and has the potential, over the coming years, to become more complex as greater legislative powers are devolved to national parliaments and assemblies. Despite recent amendments and clarifications to the law, issues around the provision of consent for treatment and medical investigations by a person with parental responsibility continue to feature in neonatal units (McKechnie and Gill, 2006). This is particularly the case if urgent decisions are required, for example, if parental consent is sought for interventions such as emergency surgery. The healthcare professional must always ensure that the father shares parental responsibility. This will not be the case if the parents are unmarried and the baby's birth has not yet been registered. Clarifying this situation may involve asking questions as sensitively as possible, in what may already be a highly stressful situation. If not handled with the requisite sensitivity, these situations can lead to the reinforcement of a view that fathers are less important than mothers, which can increase a man's sense of marginalisation.

Fathers in families

Historically a man's sense of self-identity was more often located in the public domain of work rather than the more intimate and private domain of family life (Connell, 1987; Morgan, 1992). In contrast, key areas of the study of fatherhood in recent years have focused on men's involvement with family life and the effects of wider social changes on this involvement. To emphasise some of the effects that these social changes have had upon fathers, in the following sections we examine several perspectives. The first focuses on an overview of women and mothers' roles. In the second, changes in employment and work practice and their effects upon fathers are examined. Finally the chapter concludes by beginning to consider what fathers do and do not do and their contributions to family life, a theme picked up in *Chapter 5* when we explore fatherhood in the early postnatal period.

Women and mothers' roles

Traditionally, mothers have been regarded as being homemakers with a 'woman's place' generally considered to be in the home, whilst fathers were seen as being the head of the family. Consequently, in most families, all decisions about the home and the family were made by the father. However, during the 19th century the industrial revolution brought about changes not only for society generally, but also, more specifically, within the home.

The shift of employment to towns and cities meant that fathers increasingly worked away from the home (Lewis and O'Brien, 1987; Shulman and Seiffge-Krenke, 1997; Draper, 2003). As a result, mothers increasingly took on all aspects of the day-to-day responsibilities within the home, including decisions regarding the children. Although a father usually retained his overall disciplinarian role, this was usually only enforced when he thought that the mother's authority had failed (Pleck, 1987). In many families mothers therefore became directly responsible for decisions about their child's care and early education (Lewis and O'Brien, 1987; Shulman and Seiffge-Krenke, 1997; Draper, 2003). As mothers began to assume this greater responsibility, the positive effect of a female, often more nurturing, influence on children was increasingly recognised. However, it should not be assumed that all mothers took on this nurturing role. Working class women often had to undertake paid employment, albeit often on a part-time basis, leaving their children to the care of others (Mander, 2004; Brannen and Nilsen, 2006). In upper class families both parents were often equally remote and young children were usually cared for by a nanny in a mother-substitute role. These children often saw their parents briefly and infrequently. It is also likely that in other families, the father played an integral part of the child's daily life (Burgess, 1997; Lewis and Warin, 2001). The exact situation remains unknown because of the lack of detailed documentary evidence (Jackson, 1983; Lewis and O'Brien, 1987). Therefore any generalisation should be undertaken with caution (Brannen and Nilsen, 2006).

By the early part of the 20th century changes in attitude towards women enabled them to take on new roles and responsibilities away from the home. The involvement of women in the workforce during the First World War was an important factor in women gaining the vote in 1928. This empowerment of women was also evident in their increasing access to education and the wider range of employment opportunities available to them. Greater independence and the ability to earn a reasonable wage meant that married women became less dependent on their husbands. The high level of involvement of women in the workforce during the First World War was apparent again during the Second World War.

However, whilst these factors may have led to changes for women generally, and for married women in particular, mothers retained responsibility for the day-to-day care of their children. Indeed, research in the immediate post-war period emphasised that children needed to be nurtured by their mothers and identified the harmful effects of maternal deprivation and separation (Bowlby, 1951). The view that mothers were solely responsible for the care of their children is further reflected in childcare texts from this era, which were directed exclusively at mothers. This implies that fathers were not expected to concern themselves with the care of their children. However, in more recent times it has been argued that the threat of the consequences of maternal deprivation was used as a way of oppressing women, by ensuring they stayed at home to care for their children (Billings, 1995). Those expounding the notion of maternal deprivation may also have been concerned that the retention of women in the workforce would mean a lack of employment for men returning from the Second World War. Bowlby himself subsequently amended and developed his initial theory to emphasise the importance of a consistent 'mother-figure' rather than the mother *per se*, to promote a child's wellbeing. Nevertheless, Bowlby's original work continues to be misinterpreted and, in some quarters, misused (Rutter, 1972; McFadyen, 1994).

Men's employment and work patterns

Economic support is an important way in which fathers can contribute to their child's wellbeing (Allen et al, 2007). Conversely, fathers who do not support their children in this way are much more likely to become disconnected from their child's life over time (Christensen and Palkovitz, 2001). Fatherhood can also have a positive impact on a man's working life, in that fathers can demonstrate a greater, but balanced level of commitment to their work (Eggebean and Knoester, 2001). The nature and extent of a father's employment has always had an impact on his relationship with his child. What is more difficult to determine is the exact ways in which his job, pattern of work or indeed his unemployment affects his involvement with his child.

During the 19th and early 20th century the father was generally regarded as being the head of the family and the breadwinner (Foyster, 1999). Work sometimes took fathers away from the family home and this situation became more apparent during the industrial revolution. As a consequence, fathers often became both physically and emotionally distant from their children (Lewis and O'Brien, 1987; Shulman and Seiffge-Krenke 1997; Draper, 2003). A good father during this period, was regarded as being one who provided for his family, even if this meant he worked long hours (Pleck, 1987). This link between being a good father and contributing economically to the family continues to have resonance in fathers' accounts, particularly in relation to preterm birth (Pohlman, 2005; Lindberg et al, 2007; Hugill, 2009). Although the increasing absence of working fathers from the home led to a gradual reduction of their influence on a day-to-day basis, they continued to have overall decision-making authority (Pleck, 1987). The two world wars also took most fathers away from the family home, often for long periods of time. This meant that mothers not only had to take on the day-to-day responsibility for their children, but also they became the decision-makers and providers.

A range of societal and economic changes affecting work and employment, particularly since the Second World War, has had a significant impact on fatherhood (Jackson, 1983; Burghes et al, 1997; Macfadyen et al, 2011). These include: changes in cultural and social expectations, reconfiguration of the nature and organisation of work, the increasing participation of women in further education and the workforce, the drive towards gender equality and changes in family dynamics and economic trends (Lewis and O'Brien, 1987; Bedford and Johnson, 1988; Shulman and Seiffge-Krenke, 1997; Pruett, 1998; Torr, 2003; Mander, 2004). However, a longitudinal study undertaken during the period of time covering these changes identified that a number of other factors also influenced the nature of a father's involvement in the lives of his children (Flouri and Buchanan, 2003). This study of 17 000 children born in 1958 in England, Wales and Scotland, showed that a father's educational background and employment status influenced his involvement with his children; fathers were more involved with their children if they were boys, if they were achieving academically and if they had fewer behavioural and emotional problems. Paternal health and level of maternal involvement also influenced paternal involvement. So whilst employment and patterns of work do impact upon the nature and extent of a father's involvement with his children, other factors also come into play.

Although there may still be kudos in some cultures and social groups attached to the father being the sole earner within a family, this situation has become much less evident in recent years (Brannen and Nilsen, 2006). In many families today, both the mother and father contribute to the family income, although paid employment undertaken by the mother is more likely to be fragmented and on a part-time basis (Brannen and Nilsen, 2006). After childbirth, even when both parents continue to earn income from work outside the home, fathers tend to contribute the larger income (Dermott, 2006; Johnson and Semmence, 2006). Some fathers now have more opportunties to become involved in their children's lives. In many cases, in the absence of an extended family, this occurs out of necessity to reduce childcare costs whilst the mother is working. However, in some instances maternal employment may reduce some of the pressures previously felt by fathers to provide for their families. Fathers working for more than 50 hours per week has, not unsurprisingly, a detrimental effect upon family life, particularly in terms of joint activities (Ferri and Smith, 1996). In contrast, other evidence indicates that fathers who earn more, who work shorter hours and whose partners also work, spend more time caring for their children (Smith et al, 2007). In other less common situations, the mother has become the breadwinner whilst the father has become the child's main carer.

What fathers do and do not do and their contributions to family life

What fathers do and do not do in families has an effect upon the wellbeing of their partners, children and themselves. Consequently, concern about fathers' contributions to family life is broad. Men, like women, engage in many roles in families; each is associated with a set of ideas, competencies and behaviours (Dienhart, 1998; Cabrera et al, 2000). For women, the maternal role and identity is more socially defined and ideas about the 'good mother' are deeply embedded within society (Lupton and Barclay, 1997; May, 2008). Whilst this situation can ensure the existence of a shared culture of motherhood it can also serve to limit women's lives and mothering. This situation perhaps reflects historic and enduring aspects of gender power relationships. In contrast, fatherhood is often portrayed in different terms as, 'the product of acquired knowledge and mastery of action' (Collier, 2001: 538). However, relatively little is known about how men integrate these different elements into their lives. According to Lamb (1998), fathers, unlike mothers, have historically tended to have greater latitude over their family roles. Whether men in modern times really continue to have more choice over their contribution to family life is debatable, although it has been suggested that some fathers continue to have greater leeway than mothers (Lewis, 2000; Vuori, 2009).

Given the complexity of men's lives, it is important to understand men's motivations for adopting particular roles and styles of fathering. Cabrera et al (2000) suggest that for many men the driving force behind their fathering behaviours can be traced to their childhood experiences with their own fathers and other family members, together with wider aspects of gender role and identity development. This interpretation suggests that individual models of fathering are constructed from personal experiences within a normative socially constructed frame of reference that permits and simultaneously proscribes some behaviours in preference to others. A section in the next chapter entitled, 'Modelling fatherhood', describes and contrasts some of the attempts to represent various styles of fathering and to explore how these models affect fatherhood. Increased emphasis within academic debate and policy upon men's roles in childcare reflects a change in attitude towards childcare and in the experience of fatherhood itself.

Debate about what involved fathering entails varies across national cultures and sub-cultures and is open to differing interpretations by men and women (Steinberg and Kruckman, 2000; Dermott, 2003). Despite these variations, Warin et al (1999) suggest that idealised parenting often uses as a baseline the assumption that 'good parenting' and, by extension, good fathering relates to what mothers do. There is some evidence that, in general, in recent years fathers across all social groups are becoming more active in childcare (Rustia and Abbott, 1993; Ranson, 2001; O'Brien and Shemilt, 2003; O'Brien, 2005), although this is not without personal cost to fathers (Pleck, 1997; Burgess, 2007). Perhaps reflecting this increased visibility in childcare, Yaxley et al (2005) report that stereotypical beliefs expressed by mothers about men's child-caring abilities have diminished in recent years. Consequently, fatherhood in the 21st century can be characterised by men seeking closer relationships with their children and reordering their priorities to achieve this aim, particularly in families where both parents work outside of the home (Equal Opportunities Commission, 2006). However, the same cannot be said for men's contributions to domestic work (Hochschild, 1994; Sullivan, 2000). Wajcman and Martin (2002) suggest that the erosion of gender differences in parenthood and family life may be more theoretical than reflective of the reality of men and women's everyday lives.

While the numbers are still few, more men are becoming the primary carer of their children while their partners work outside the home often, but not exclusively, in high profile or highly remunerated employment. A Canadian study (Doucet, 2006) sought to explore men's roles in the home from the perspective of a group of men who were self-declared primary child carers in their families. This study included in depth interviews with over 60 fathers from a diverse range of social circumstances out of a total sample of over 100; other data collection methods included focus groups in internet-based interactions. Doucet's (2006) analysis reveals some interesting insights into how even highly involved men view childcare. Despite considerable similarities between mothers' and fathers' childcare routines and activities, fathers in her study continued to differentiate fathering as distinct from what mothers did. Grossman et al (1999) suggest that many fathers place considerable emphasis upon developing friendship with their child, being together, doing things together and teaching the child independence. These features of parenting behaviour seem to be important elements of masculine constructions of childcare (Easterbrooks and Goldberg, 1984; Brandth and Kvande, 1998). If this is the case, then this interpretation serves to distinguish fathers' childcare activities as distinct from and yet synergistic with those of mothers. It could mark a counterbalance to using maternal activities alone as the standard reference of childcare and contradicts ideas that 'good parenting' consists of gender-neutral behaviours based upon 'good mothering'.

When fathers become the primary carer they often struggle to reconcile this status with their existing ideas about manliness (Doucet, 2006). Doucet (2006) reported in her study that fathers often sought out opportunities to express their notions of masculine behaviour. These activities ranged from engaging in sport activities, continuing to work part-time and becoming involved in local community activities. Additional evidence regarding fathers' concern about the relatively lower status of childcare comes from Warin et al's (1999) study into how British fathers sought to balance their employment and family life. They concluded that for some men the world of work was more attractive than greater involvement in family life and suggested that this might be because work afforded them a higher status yet was at the same time less emotionally demanding than family life. These findings may have resonance with fathers who opt to take on additional childcare responsibilities.

In the UK, considerable public and media attention has been paid to non-resident and absent fathers and the apparent links to poor childhood outcome. However, there is little unequivocal evidence attributing poor academic achievement, sex role and gender identity development directly to the absence of a father (Burghes et al, 1997; Cabrera et al, 2000). Even though fathers may be absent for long periods of time they might have considerable impact on their children (Burgess, 1997). Consequently, debate about the effects of absent fathers on their children remains problematic without first considering why these men are absent from the home and what mothers are saying and doing about such absence. It may have more to do, for example, with economic loss, existing social disadvantage or parental conflict, and requires more empirical study before cause and effect can be directly attributed.

Beginning in 1999 as the 'Fathers Direct programme' and now known as the 'Fatherhood Institute' a small charity was established that sought to promote more involved fathering and co-operative parenting (Burgess, 2007). In 2007, as part of the organisation's aim to promote greater inclusion of fathers, it published a guide for maternity service staff detailing practical measures they could take to facilitate this (Fatherhood Institute, 2007). Currently, the Fatherhood Institute is engaged in high profile lobbying for better recognition of fathers in national polices, in providing research-based advice and information to fathers, families and professionals, and in offering training. Many contemporary accounts of fatherhood express an apparent ideology of shared parenting; however, there remain considerable cultural and social prohibitions which continue to exclude fathers from having equity (Equal Opportunities Commission, 2007).

Increased participation by fathers in childcare and domestic activities is often inferred as supporting improved family life. However, there is limited unambiguous empirical evidence to support this assertion; much of the evidence for men's greater contribution and participation in domesticity is lacking (Matheson and Summerfield, 2001; Vuori, 2009). It seems that, despite evidence of fathers' increased presence in the home and of women in employment, mothers continue to be the major contributors to domestic work and childcare (Hochschild, 1994; Matheson and Summerfield, 2001). The reasons behind this are complex and reflect many different facets of and tensions within modern parenting. Furthermore, there is a significant body of evidence that for some women and families, the father's presence can be harmful, having short and long-term detrimental effects on women and their children's emotional and physical wellbeing (Jaffe et al, 2003; Steen-Greaves et al, 2009; Brown et al, 2011; Smith-Stover et al, 2011).

Sadly, not all children are healthy and some will have chronic illness or life-limiting conditions. In these situations, children often need additional levels of care beyond that seen with healthy children. Caring for a child in these circumstances, whether at home or in hospital, is taxing for all family members. Illness in children complicates routine activities and makes them more time-consuming, economically burdensome and emotionally wearing. While some parents adapt readily, others find these additional burdens and loss of control less easy to cope with. Despite these additional demands upon parents, Chesler and Parry (2001) reported that some mothers sought to moderate fathers' contributions to childcare, preferring instead to do it themselves. This finding echoes the reports of maternal gatekeeping behaviour seen in other circumstances (Allen and Hawkins, 1999; Gavin et al, 2002; Yaxley et al, 2005; Schoppe-Sullivan et al, 2008). A further study added insight suggesting that sometimes fathers themselves see their role as primarily providing respite for their partner (Sullivan-Bolyai et al, 2006). In contrast, more recent accounts tend to report increased father involvement in childcare replicating what is seen more generally (McNeil, 2007; Hobson and Noyes, 2011; Swallow et al, 2011). Furthermore, Hobson and Noyes (2011) suggest that some fathers are able to capitalise on the opportunities afforded by their difficult situation and build more positive and robust relationships with their children and partners. Clearly the involvement and contributions of fathers whose children experience poor health is highly contextual and while it is notable that there are similarities between these fathers and fatherhood in other situations, further empirical study is required, and any generalisations should be treated with caution.

While this book is concerned with fatherhood around the time of birth and early infancy it is important to emphasise that fatherhood roles continue to evolve across the whole life course. Fathers and their relationships with their adolescent and adult children have received limited research attention and what there is has tended to focus on problematic situations (Stelle and Sheehan, 2011). What little non-problem focused research there is suggests that many fathers seem comfortable on the sidelines of adolescent family life (Shulman and Seiffge-Krenke, 1997), engaging preferentially in the traditional role of 'provider' which speculatively affords them a channel for their feelings of emotional attachment to their family (Christiansen and Palkovitz, 2001).

Fatherhood across the life course can be characterised as a continual and never-ending cycle of negotiation and renegotiation of new and existing relationships and roles. In effect, fathers, mothers and their children co-construct their relationships over time (Stelle and Sheehan, 2011), the beginnings of which are seen during pregnancy, childbirth and early infancy. These negotiations are influenced by a great many factors, both private and public. For example, paternity leave arrangements and workplace policies and practices all affect fathers' opportunities to contribute to family life. Whereas, on a private level, individual aspiration for fatherhood, and choices tempered by the expectations of others, are also influential.

Conclusion

This chapter has explored a number of concerns with regard to understanding the practice and meanings of fatherhood. Despite attempts to pin down a definition of fatherhood it remains a somewhat imprecise concept. The practices of fathering and the experiences of fatherhood have been affected by significant social changes, with the result that modern ideas about fatherhood are perhaps more defined by their diversity than by their adherence to stereotypical ideas about how fathers should and actually do engage in family life.

It is clear that there are many ways to be a father and that fatherhood has biological, social, political and legal dimensions to it. As we shall see in the coming chapters, many of these facets of fatherhood have become topics for empirical research, public discussion and political debate.

Key points

- Despite having increased visibility, fatherhood remains a somewhat diverse and complex concept
- Modern fatherhood can be characterised by the durability and reinterpretation of older ideas into emerging ideas about how men should conduct themselves in families
- Ideas about what fatherhood means are related to our culturally determined understandings of gender roles and concepts of masculinity, and these influence the law, politics and the realities of everyday life for fathers
- If a child's parents are married at the time of the child's birth, they will both automatically have parental responsibility. Fathers who are not married to the child's mother can acquire parental responsibility, but this must be done by including their name on the child's birth certificate
- Recent political reforms and wider social changes have sought to maintain men's economic responsibilities for their children whilst simultaneously eroding existing gender-based hierarchies around work and childcare

---

Case history
Fatherhood experiences

Sue, Mary and Fiona are maternity healthcare professionals and Diane is a student. Over 35 years separates their respective ages. During a break they are reflecting about some recent encounters with fathers and this provokes them to reminisce about some of their own experiences.

Diane: 'I find talking to some fathers a lot more difficult than talking to mothers. With the mothers there is more in common and they open up more than fathers.'
Fiona: 'Don't you just hate it when some of these dads come in armed with all these ideas and want to take over, they've been to a couple of antenatal classes, read a few books and internet downloads and think they know it all.'
Mary: 'Yes, it can be a bit in your face, but I think it's really nice when they show an interest, at least it shows they care, I know my own dad loved to be involved.'
Fiona: 'I don't know why they want to get so involved, it's not right for them to see everything that is going on and they have no reason to be as emotional as the mothers who have given birth. It used to be much better when they only visited in the evenings and we could spend the whole day with the mothers, not like now when they are either hanging around all day or in and out like yoyos.'
Mary: 'I remember that my Barry was great with the kids when they were growing up; when I was in work he would do everything, except clean the bathroom [laughing]. My dad was the same with me when I was younger, he was very hands on, even before it was popular.'
Sue: 'You might just be lucky, I never saw my dad much in the week, he was always at work except for high days and holidays and even then he didn't know what to do with us or how to talk to us; he left everything to our mother.'
Fiona [after a short silence]: 'I used to blame my dad a bit when I was younger, he wasn't very good, well, you know, a bit distant and unemotional but then maybe his dad wasn't very good, either.'
Mary [with a smile on her face]: 'Yeah but that was quite a while ago, Fiona.'

Reflective questions

* What factors may have led these members of the healthcare team to think about fathers in the ways they do?
* What might be the effects of these points of view upon fathers' experiences?

> * To what extent do the beliefs and experiences in this scenario reflect or counter your own experience of fathers and being fathered?
> * What strategies could be implemented to challenge some of the assumptions made about fathers that feature in this scenario in your practice area?

References

Adoption and Children Act 2002. Available from: http:www.legislation.gov.uk/ukpga/2002/38/c (accessed 25 March 2012)

Allen S, Daly K with Father Involvement Research Alliance (2007) *The effects of father involvement: An updated research summary of the evidence.* Centre for Families, Work and Well-Being, Guelph ON

Allen SM, Hawkins AJ (1999) Maternal gate keeping: Mothers' beliefs and behaviours that inhibit greater father involvement in family work. *Journal of Marriage and the Family* **61**(1): 199–212.

Bedford VA, Johnson N (1988) The role of the father. *Midwifery* **4**(4): 190–5

Billings JR (1995) Bonding theory: Tying mothers in knots? A critical review of the application of a theory to nursing. *Journal of Clinical Nursing* **4**(4): 207–11

Bowlby J (1951) *Maternal care and maternal mental health.* World Health Organization, Geneva

Brandth B, Kvande E (1998) Masculinity and childcare: The reconstruction of fathering. *Sociological Review* **46**(2): 293–313

Brannen J, Nilsen A (2006) From fatherhood to fathering: Transmission and change among British fathers in four generation families. *Sociology* **40**(2): 335–52.

Brown G, Brady G, Letherby G (2011) Young mothers' experiences of power, control and violence within intimate and familial relationships. *Child Care in Practice* **17**(4): 359–74

Burgess A (1997) *Fatherhood reclaimed: The making of the modern father.* Vermillion, London

Burgess A (2007) *The costs and benefits of active fatherhood: Evidence and insights to inform the development of policy and practice.* Fathers Direct, London

Burghes L, Clarke L, Cronin N (1997) *Fathers and fatherhood in Britain.* Family Policy Study Centre, London

Cabrera NJ, Tamis-LeMonda CS, Bradley RH, Hofferth S, Lamb ME (2000) Fatherhood in the twenty-first century. *Child Development* **71**(1): 127–36

Children Act 1989. Available from: http:www.legislation.gov.uk/ukpga/1989/41/c (accessed 25 March 2012)

Child Support Act 1991. Available from: http:www.legislation.gov.uk/ukpga/1991/48/c

(accessed 25 March 2012)

Chesler MA, Parry C (2001) Gender roles and/or styles in crisis: An integrative analysis of the experiences of fathers of children with cancer. *Qualitative Health Research* **11**: 363–84

Christiansen SL, Palkovitz R (2001) Why the 'good provider' role still matters: Providing as a form of paternal involvement. *Journal of Family Issues* **22**(1): 84–106

Collier R (2001) A hard time to be a father? Reassessing the relationship between law, policy, and family (practices). *Journal of Law and Society* **28**(4): 520–45

Collier R (2002) Masculinities. *Sociology* **36**(3): 737–42

Collinson D, Hearn J (1996) 'Men' at 'work': Multiple masculinities/multiple work-places. In: Mac A, Ghaill M (eds) *Understanding masculinities: Social relations and cultural arenas.* Open University Press, Buckingham

Connell RW (1987) *Gender and power: Society, the person and sexual politics.* Polity Press, Cambridge

Connell RW (1995) *Masculinities.* Polity Press, Cambridge

Connell RW (2005) *Masculinities* (2nd edn). Polity Press, London

Connell RW, Messerschmidt JW (2005) Hegemonic masculinity: Rethinking the concept. *Gender and Society* **19**(6): 829–59.

Department for Work and Pensions (2007) Available from: http://statistics.dwp.gov.uk/asd/asd1/child_support/index.php?page=csa_quarterly_dec07 (accessed 27 March 2012)

Dermott E (2003) The intimate father: Defining paternal involvement. *Sociological Research Online* **8**(4). Available from: http://www.socresonline.org.uk/8/4/dermott.html. (accessed 20 February 2012)

Dermott E (2006) What's parenthood got to do with it? Men's hours of paid work. *British Journal of Sociology* **57**(4): 619–34.

Dienhart A (1998) *Reshaping fatherhood: The social construction of shared parenting.* Sage, Thousand Oaks CA

Doucet A (2206) *Do men mother? Fatherhood, care and domestic responsibility.* University of Toronto Press, Toronto ON

Draper H (2007) Paternity fraud and compensation for misattributed paternity. *Journal of Medical Ethics* **33**(8): 475–80

Draper J (2003) Men's passage to fatherhood: An analysis of the contemporary relevance of transition theory. *Nursing Inquiry* **10**(1): 66–78

Duncombe J, Marsden D (1998) 'Stepford wives' and 'hollow men'? Doing emotion work, doing gender and 'authenticity' in intimate heterosexual relationships. In: Bendelow G, Williams SJ (eds) *Emotions in social life.* Routledge, London

Duncombe J, Marsden D (1999) Love and intimacy: The gender division of emotion and 'emotion work': A neglected aspect of sociological discussion of heterosexual rela-tionships. In: Allan G (ed) *The sociology of the family: A reader.* Blackwell, Oxford

Easterbrooks MA, Goldberg WA (1984) Toddler development in the family: Impact of father involvement and parenting characteristics. *Child Development* **55**: 740–52.

Eggebean DJ, Knoester C (2001) Does fatherhood matter for men? *Journal of Marriage and the Family Issues* **63**: 381–93

Equal Opportunities Commission (2006) *Twenty-first century dad*. Equal Opportunities Commission, Manchester

Equal Opportunities Commission (2007) *The state of the modern family*. Equal Opportunities Commission, Manchester

Family Law Reform Act 1987. Available from: http:www.legislation.gov.uk/ukpga/1987/42/c (accessed 25 March 2012)

Fatherhood Institute (2007) *Including new fathers: A guide for maternity professionals*. Fatherhood institute, London

Ferri E, Smith K (1996) *Parenting in the 1990s*. Family Polices Study Centre & Joseph Rowntree Foundation, London & York

Finn M, Henwood K (2009) Exploring masculinities within men's identificatory imaginings of first-time fatherhood. *British Journal of Social Psychology* **48**: 547–62

Flouri E, Buchanan A (2003) What predicts fathers' involvement with their children? A prospective study of intact families. *British Journal of Developmental Psychology* **21**: 81–98

Foyster EA (1999) *Manhood in early modern England: Honour, sex and marriage*. Longman, London

Gavin LE, Black MM, Minor S, Abel Y, Papas M, Bentley M (2002) Young disadvantaged fathers involvement with their infants. *Journal of Adolescent Health* **31**: 266–76

Grossman KE, Grossman K, Zimmermann P (1999) A wider view of attachment and exploration: Stability and change during the years of immaturity. In: Cassidy J, Shaver PR (eds) *Handbook of attachment: Theory, research, and clinical applications*. Guilford Press, New York NY

Hearn J (1992) *Men in the public eye: The construction and deconstruction of public men and public patriarchies*. Routledge, London

Hearn J (1996) Is masculinity dead? A critique of the concept of masculinity/masculinities. In: Mac A, Ghaill M (eds) *Understanding masculinities: Social relations and cultural arenas*. Open University Press, Buckingham

Hearn J (2004) From hegemonic masculinity to the hegemony of men. *Feminist Theory* **5**(1): 49–72

Hobson L, Noyes J (2011) Fatherhood and children with complex healthcare needs: Qualitative study of fathering, caring and parenting. *BMC Nursing* **10**(5): doi:10.1186/1472-6955-10-5

Hochschild AR (1994) The second shift: Employed women are putting in another day of work at home. In: Kimmel MS, Messner MA (eds) *Men's lives* (3rd edn). Allyn and Bacon, Needham Heights MA

Hugill K (2009) *The experiences and emotion work of fathers in a neonatal unit.* Unpublished PhD thesis. University of Central Lancashire, Preston

Jackson B (1983) *Fatherhood.* George Allen & Unwin, London

Jaffe SR, Moffitt TE, Caspi A, Taylor A (2003) Life with (or without) father: The benefits of living with two biological parents depend on the father's antisocial behaviour. *Child Development* **74**(1): 109–26

Johnson G, Semmence J (eds) (2006) *Individual income 1996/97–2004/05.* Office for National Statistics, London

Lamb ME (1998) Fatherhood then and now. In: Booth, A, Crouther AC (eds) *Men in families: When do they get involved? What difference does it make?* Lawrence Erlbaum Associates, London

Lewis C (2000) *A man's place in the home: Fathers and families in the UK.* Family Policy Study Centre & Joseph Rowntree Foundation, London and York

Lewis C, O'Brien M (1987) What good are dads? *Father Facts* **1**: 1–12

Lewis C, Warin J (2001) Constraints on fathers: Research, history and clinical practice. In: Lewis C, O'Brien M (eds) *Reassessing fatherhood.* Sage, London

Lindberg B, Axelsson K, Öhrling K (2007) The birth of premature infants: Experiences from the fathers' perspective. *Journal of Neonatal Nursing* **13**(4): 142–9

Lupton D, Barclay L (1997) *Constructing fatherhood: Discourses and experiences.* Sage, London

McFadyen A (1994) *Special care babies and their developing relationships.* Routledge, London

Macfadyen A, Swallow V, Santacroce S, Lambert H (2011) Involving fathers in research. *Journal for Specialists in Pediatric Nursing* **16**: 216–9

McKechnie L, Gill AB (2006) Consent for neonatal research. *Archives of Disease in Childhood Fetal and Neonatal Edition* **91**(3): F374–6

McNeil T (2007) Fathers of children with a chronic health condition: Beyond gender stereotypes. *Men and Masculinities* **9**(4): 409-424

McVeigh K (2007) Stockbroker wins £22,000 damages for paternity deceit. *The Guardian.* Available from: http://www.guardian.co.uk/uk/2007/apr/04/law.world/print (accessed 23 January 2012)

Mander R (2004) *Men and maternity.* Routledge, London

Matheson J, Summerfield C (eds) (2001) *Social focus on men.* Office for National Statistics, London

May V (2008) On being a 'good mother': The moral presentation of self in written life stories. *Sociology* **42**(3): 470–86

Morgan DHJ (1992) *Discovering men.* Routledge, London

Mugai C (1999) Affect, imagery and attachment: Working models of interpersonal affect and the socialisation of emotion. In: Cassidy J, Shaver PR (eds) *Handbook of attachment: Theory, research, and clinical applications.* Guilford Press, New York NY

O'Brien M (2005) *Shared caring: Bringing fathers into the frame, EOC Working Paper Series 18.* Equal Opportunities Commission, Manchester

O'Brien M, Shemilt I (2003) *Working fathers: Earning and caring research discussion series.* Equal Opportunities Commission, Manchester

Pleck JH (1987) American fathering in historical perspective. In: Kimmel MS (ed) *Changing men: New directions in research on men and masculinity.* Sage, Newbury Park CA

Pleck JH (1997) Paternal involvement: Levels, sources and consequences. In: Lamb ME (ed) *The role of the father in child development* (3rd edn). Wiley, New York NY

Pohlman S (2005) The primacy of work and fathering preterm infants: Findings from an interpretive phenomenological study. *Advances in Neonatal Care* **5**: 204–16

Pruett KD (1998) Role of the father. *Pediatrics* **102**(5): 1253–61

Ranson G (2001) Men at work: Change – or no change: In the era of the 'new father'. *Men and Masculinities* **4**(3): 3–26

Rustia J, Abbott D (1993) Father involvement in infant care: Two longitudinal studies. *International Journal of Nursing Studies* **30**(6): 467–76

Rutter M (1972) *Maternal deprivation reassessed.* Routledge, London

Schoppe-Sullivan SJ, Cannon EA, Brown GL, Mansgelsdorf SC, Szewczyk Sokolowski M (2008) Maternal gatekeeping, coparenting quality, and fathering behaviour in families with infants. *Journal of Family Psychology* **22**(3): 389–98

Segal L (1997) *Slow motion: Changing masculinities, changing men* (2nd edn). Virago, London

Seidler VJ (1997) *Man enough: Embodying masculinities.* Sage, London

Seidler VJ (2007) Masculinities, bodies, and emotional life. *Men and Masculinities* **10**(1): 9–21

Shulman S, Seiffge-Krenke I (1997) *Fathers and adolescents.* Penguin, Harmondsworth

Smiler AP (2004) Thirty years after the discovery of gender: Psychological concepts and measures of masculinity. *Sex Roles: A Journal of Research* **50**(1–2): 15–26

Smith A, Morton S, Wasoff F (2007) *Working fathers in Europe, earning and caring? CRFR Research Briefing 30.* Centre for Research on Families and Relationships, Edinburgh

Smith-Stover C, McMahon TJ, Easton C (2011) The impact of fatherhood on treatment response for men with co-occurring alcohol dependence and intimate partner violence. *American Journal of Drug and Alcohol Abuse* **37**: 74–8

Steen-Greaves M, Downe S, Graham-Kevan N (2009) Men and women's perceptions and experiences of attending managing abusive behaviour programme. *Evidence Based Midwifery* **7**(4) 128–35

Stelle CD, Sheehan NW (2011) Exploring paternal maturity in the relationship between older fathers and adult children. *International Journal of Aging and Human Development* **72**(1): 45–65

Steinberg S, Kruckman L (2000) Reinventing fatherhood in Japan and Canada. *Social Science and Medicine* **50**(9): 1257–72

Sullivan-Bolyai S, Rosenburg R, Bayard M (2006) Fathers' reflections on parenting young children with type 1 diabetes. *American Journal of Maternal Child Health* **31**(1): 24–31

Sullivan O (2000) The division of domestic labour. *Sociology* **34**(3): 437–56

Swallow V, Lambert H, Santacroce S, Macfadyen A (2011) Fathers and mothers developing skills in managing children's long-term medical conditions: How do their qualitative accounts compare? *Child: Care Health and Development* **37**(4): 512–23

Torr J (2003) *Is there a father in the house?* Radcliffe Medical Press, Abingdon

Vuori J (2009) Men's choices and masculine duties: Fathers in expert discussions. *Men and Masculinities* **12**(1): 45–72

Wajcman J, Martin B (2002) Narratives of identity in modern management: The corrosion of gender difference? *Sociology* **36**(4): 985–1002

Warin J, Solomon Y, Lewis C, Langford W (1999) *Fathers, work and family life.* Family Polices Study Centre & Joseph Rowntree Foundation, London & York

Webb J (2008) The legislative and policy context of young fathers and their children. In: Reeves J (ed) *Inter-professional approaches to young fathers.* M&K Update Ltd, Keswick

Woodhill BM, Samuels CA (2004) Desirable and undesirable androgyny: A prescription for the twenty-first century. *Journal of Gender Studies* **13**(1):15–28

Woollett A, Nicolson P (1998) The social construction of motherhood and fatherhood. In: Niven CA, Walker A (eds) *Current Issues in Infancy and Parenthood 3.* Butterworth Heinemann, Oxford

Yaxley D, Vinter L, Young V (2005) *Dads and their babies: The mothers' perspective, EOC Working paper series 41.* Equal Opportunities Commission, Manchester

Chapter 3

Becoming a father: Reconciling realities

Merryl Harvey and Kevin Hugill

Introduction

Within this chapter, the realities of becoming and being a father are explored. The chapter begins by considering some of the ideas about men's transition to fatherhood; when and how this happens, the feelings it engenders and the factors that may impact upon the process. We then review different perspectives on the ways in which fathers make emotional connections with their children and the factors that may hinder or facilitate this process. This is followed by a review of the different models of fatherhood and more specifically what fathers do in families, or perhaps more importantly, do not do. We then seek to reconcile the everyday realities of fatherhood by considering what happens when this occurs in less favourable circumstances; when a father experiences depression or mental illness. We also consider the experiences of young fathers and some of the factors that may impinge on young fatherhood. The chapter concludes with two case histories and activities to facilitate reflection on current and future practice.

Ideas about the transition to fatherhood

The transition to fatherhood is a milestone in a man's life and can affect his identity and self-esteem; consequently, it is often more challenging than is anticipated (Barclay and Lupton, 1999; Reeves, 2006; Genesoni and Tallandini, 2009). Men and women go through a process of transition in becoming parents although the exact beginning, sequencing and duration of this process are thought to differ between the sexes (Smith, 1999).

According to Henderson and Brouse (1991) men go through a series of transitional stages as they develop their fatherhood identities and roles. These stages can be characterised as beginning with abstract preconceptions and moving on to more substantial and concrete understandings embedded in the everyday realties of fatherhood. Perhaps wisely, timescales are not offered for this transition; this leaves unanswered an important question, when does transition to fatherhood begin? For some men it can be when the decision is made to have a child, for others it may begin on confirmation of the pregnancy or when they see their unborn child during an ultrasound scan (Draper, 2002a, 2002b). For some men, transition to fatherhood begins with the birth of their child, whilst others may feel that it does not start until after the baby has arrived. However, it seems that for most men transition to fatherhood begins at some undefined point during the pregnancy.

Whenever it begins, the phrase often used in the literature to describe becoming a father is that it is 'life-changing' (Deave and Johnson, 2008; Fägerskiöld, 2008). Part of the process of transition involves a man thinking about what kind of a father he wants to be (Condon, 2006; Reeves, 2006). This in turn can bring pressures and expectations, which may be self-imposed or created by family, friends or society more generally. For some fathers, self-imposed pressures arise from the desire to replicate their own experiences of being fathered whilst others want to be a better father to their children than their own father had been to them (St John et al, 2005; Tyrer et al, 2005; Hugill, 2009). The more limited social and psychological preparation and support available for new fathers during the perinatal period, particularly in comparison to the provision for new mothers, often adds to the challenge.

Transition to fatherhood involves taking on new roles, developing existing skills and mastering new ones. For many men, the challenges associated with adjusting to the roles and responsibilities of fatherhood include trying to maintain a work and life balance whilst coping with financial pressures, role uncertainty and changes in relationships generally, and with their partner in particular (McVeigh et al, 2002; Deave and Johnson, 2008; Bateman and Bharj, 2009; Genesoni and Tallandini, 2009). These challenges can invoke negative feelings of low self-esteem and some men may feel a lack of control over their lives in ways that they may not have previously experienced. Factors that can impact on transition to fatherhood are identified in a longitudinal study of men's adaptation. Fathers who were younger, had a shorter relationship with their partner and who were in part-time employment had the highest levels of distress (Buist et al, 2003). Levels of paternal distress were highest at 24 to 26 weeks' gestation (Buist et al, 2003). This finding may be of particular significance for fathers who experience preterm birth around this time. More extreme cases of paternal distress during the perinatal period can lead to significant and longer-term mental health problems (Department of Health, 2009a). It appears, then, that transition to fatherhood can be a stressful time for some, and is perhaps more complex than is sometimes supposed. In more extreme cases it can be a time of crisis (Tiller, 1995; Henwood and Procter, 2003). This might be more likely to be the case if the pregnancy was unplanned or if problems arise regarding the mother's or baby's health during the pregnancy (Buist et al, 2003). Other less direct factors may also impinge on a father's transition to fatherhood in a negative way such as employment or housing difficulties or health problems of other family members or friends.

However, transition to fatherhood can also be a happy and optimistic time. Fatherhood may engender men's positive feelings about themselves, manifested in greater self-confidence, sensitivity and self-worth and increased empathy with others. Fatherhood can also bring a purpose, structure and security to a man's life (Jackson, 1983; Dartnell et al, 2005; Reeves, 2006; World Health Organization, 2007). For some men, fatherhood enables them to establish and be part of a family for the first time (Letherby et al, 2004; Tyrer et al, 2005). Many men relish the challenges and responsibilities that fatherhood brings and enjoy the recognition of their new role by others (Dartnell et al, 2005; St John et al, 2005). Fatherhood can also strengthen a man's relationship with his partner and other family members (Fägerskiöld, 2008; Premberg et al, 2008). For some men, becoming a father prompts changes to lifestyle, behaviour and attitudes that were not triggered to the same extent by their partner, other family members or society more generally (St John et al, 2005; Premberg et al, 2008). A study by Foster (2004) provides a more extreme example of this whereby men living in violent and impoverished communities felt fatherhood made them more aware of their own mortality.

Given the roles and responsibilities that new fathers face, it is not surprising that men have often described experiencing a rollercoaster of emotions as they adjust to becoming a father. Joy, pride and feelings of self-worth are often mixed with feeling overwhelmed, detached, excluded and weighed down by the prospect of their ongoing responsibilities (Draper, 2003; Deave and Johnson, 2008; Fägerskiöld, 2008). Indeed men have said that they would like more guidance during pregnancy on how to cope with fatherhood (Singh and Newburn, 2000; McElliot, 2001) and they are more likely to be receptive to this type of information, guidance and support during this time (Fagan et al, 2007). It is open to debate as to who is best placed to support new fathers during their transition to fatherhood. Whilst a number of different healthcare professional groups are involved in maternity and early newborn care, few regard the father as being their priority at this time. Indeed, some healthcare professionals involved in perinatal care do not feel that supporting fathers is part of their role at all (Harvey, 2010). Perhaps this message is conveyed in some way to fathers and is part of the reason why many fathers do not attend antenatal parentcraft classes (Redshaw et al, 2007; Mottram, 2008).

Several studies have reported that prospective fathers sometimes describe experiencing a patronising or marginalising attitude whilst attending antenatal parenting classes and pregnancy screening (Henwood and Procter, 2003; Bradley et al, 2004; Locock and Alexander, 2006) and this may affect their participation. This perspective is endorsed by one father's experience: 'They were so boring; nothing that wasn't in the books already and one midwife was so snotty, you could see she didn't want us [fathers] there. She only talked at the women and even talked down to [a] woman who asked a stupid question' (Hugill, 2009: 135). Consequently, many fathers who do attend classes often feel that they do not meet their needs (Deave and Johnson, 2008; Premberg et al, 2008). In addition, this resource is often only available for those who are able to cover the economic costs of attendance. Fathers have also reported difficulty attending antenatal appointments and classes due to work commitments (Deave and Johnson, 2008; Mottram, 2008) and there is often confusion and uncertainty over a father's entitlement to attend these during work time (Chin et al, 2011; Direct Gov UK, 2011). The lack of healthcare professional support for new fathers becomes even more of an issue for fathers who are finding transition to fatherhood difficult or who become fathers in less usual circumstances, such as following preterm birth. Their concerns can go unrecognised because the mother and the baby are usually the focus of everyone's attention (Buist et al, 2003).

Making emotional connections

Fatherhood usually brings about a psychological response which triggers the development of an emotional connection or bond with the baby. Developing an emotional connection with a child is generally regarded as being an important aspect of being a 'good' parent (Barclay and Lupton, 1999). This emotional connection has become enshrined in what we now refer to as 'attachment theory' (Bowlby, 1988, 2005). Ideas informing this theory, originally described by Bowlby in the late 1950s, appeared in the seminal report, *Maternal care and mental health,* for the World Health Organization which was later presented in book form as *Child care and the growth of love* (Bowlby, 2005). Much of the literature regarding attachment theory focuses on the role of the mother. As is the case in other parenting research, fathers are under-represented in parent–infant attachment literature (Mercer and Ferketich, 1990; Condon et al, 2008). However, some insight has been provided into the ways in which a father forms an emotional connection with his child and the implications associated with this process (Bretherton et al, 2005). Many fathers begin to feel affection for their baby during their partner's pregnancy regardless of how their baby was conceived (Hjelmstedt et al, 2007). Whilst they experience the pregnancy second-hand, fathers can feel and sometimes see their baby move in utero and can listen to the heart beat. Seeing the baby during the ultrasound scan is also important when the child often seems real for the first time (Bondas-Salonen, 1998; Draper, 2003). Studies by Draper (2002a, 2002b) showed that pregnancy confirmation and being present during the ultrasound scan enable fathers to visualise the pregnancy in a tangible way and have a positive impact on his feelings for his baby. However, the father's background and previous experiences may have an effect on the nature and extent of his feelings for his child in a more general way.

Fathers often say their feelings for their baby strengthen as the pregnancy progresses (Hjelmstedt et al, 2007). This has implications for those who experience miscarriage, stillbirth and preterm birth (Puddifoot and Johnson, 1999; McCreight, 2004; Turton et al, 2006). A father's feelings for his unborn child may manifest as concern about the health of the baby during the pregnancy. However, fathers often hide these fears from their partner (Smith, 1998). Fathers may also experience disruption to attachment processes similar to that shown in mothers when preterm birth occurs (Richards, 1983; McFadyen, 1994). Problems that occur during pregnancy that may impinge on the child's wellbeing have the potential to influence father–infant attachment. However, there is inconsistency in the literature regarding the impact of pregnancy-related problems. A longitudinal study comparing the impact of high and low-risk pregnancies found that at one week post-delivery there was no difference in the attachment scores of fathers who experienced either type of pregnancy (Mercer and Ferketich, 1990). Whilst this appears to suggest that risk status did not influence paternal–infant attachment, more of the high-risk fathers had other children. This may have influenced their attachment with the current child. This study also found that mothers had significantly higher scores than their partners (Mercer and Ferketich, 1990). However, the opposite effect has been reported in another study in which fathers had higher scores than their partners (White et al, 1999). There are a number of variables that may influence the findings of these and other similar studies, for example, prior experience of high-risk pregnancy, the way in which the high-risk pregnancies were managed and underlying paternal/maternal anxiety.

Many fathers regard attending the birth of their child as being a rite of passage which confirms that they are now a father (Jackson et al, 2003; Lundqvist and Jakobsson, 2003). Witnessing the birth may also be an important factor in the development of father–infant attachment (Klaus and Kennell, 1982; Bowen and Miller, 1980). Although this view is contentious, this has implications for fathers who do not attend their child's birth, for whatever reason. Mothers and fathers elicit similar nurturing behaviours in the early neonatal period when they can be

39

observed touching, stroking and exploring their baby (Klaus and Kennell, 1982; Jackson, 1983; Lamb, 1997). Some mammalian animal studies have shown that immediately after birth, physical contact between parents and their offspring enhances attachment, although this is not the case in all species. Allied to this is the notion of a sensitive period of time during which physical contact should be made between parent and child. Whilst the extent to which these findings apply across other populations and species must be questioned, the concept of a sensitive period has been subsequently endorsed by researchers studying human behaviour (Klaus et al, 1972). Although the original study was small-scale, involving only 28 mothers, and was insufficiently validated (Richards, 1983; Mercer and Ferketich, 1990; Billings, 1995) it has, despite methodological and conceptual limitations, remained influential within maternity care.

The claim that contact with the baby during the first few hours after birth enhanced mother–infant attachment led to the widescale implementation of 'rooming-in' in maternity units during the 1970s (Klaus and Kennell 1982; Roeber, 1987). Providing opportunities for mothers to hold their baby, particularly if born preterm, has a significant effect upon mother and infant interactions, emotional wellbeing and attachment (Flacking et al, 2006; Riikka Korjaa et al, 2008). The importance of early physical contact appears to be endorsed by fathers who reported that the sooner they held their baby, the sooner they felt love for their child (Sullivan, 1999) and that after holding they felt more emotionally connected to their child (Lundqvist and Jakobsson, 2003). The notion of a sensitive period also appears to be supported by the literature exploring the long-term negative impact of parent–infant separation (Bowlby, 1988; Field, 2007). Alternatively, failure to form an attachment after separation may be a self-fulfilling prophecy (Billings, 1995). It is also possible that it is the anxiety about the cause of the separation, rather than the separation itself that inhibits parents' ability to form an attachment with their child (Meadows, 1986).

The ways in which parents, and fathers in particular, form an emotional connection with their child is clearly a complex process that involves physiological, sociological and psychological factors (Boulton, 1983). Whilst there is a lack of consensus regarding the process, it would appear that external factors can be influential. It should be noted, however, that many studies exploring parent–infant attachment rely on self-report data, which participants may be tempted to manipulate to be regarded as being a 'good' parent. It is also the case that for most theories of attachment, there is a counter-argument. Such counter-arguments are supported by evidence that many fathers who successfully establish an attachment with their baby who did not attend the birth of their child, including adoptive fathers, those who have a child through surrogacy and those who were fathers of newborn infants requiring hospital care in the era of restricted visiting.

Models of fatherhood and what fathers do

We have explored factors that may influence transition to fatherhood and the ways in which a father forms an emotional connection with his baby. What constitutes a father's role once his child is born? In the past, fatherhood was often considered in terms of responsibility, control and duty, with limited emphasis placed upon childcare and family life; this situation has altered considerably since the Victorian era. The changing roles, responsibilities and expectations of fathers in modern times in the UK can be captured in different models of fatherhood. Brannen and Nilsen (2006) described three such models: 'work-focused fathers', 'family men' and 'hands-on fathers'. If viewed together, these three models describe a shift in focus over time. At one end of the continuum is the breadwinner and the perhaps more remote father of the 'work-focused' model. More centrally placed in the 'family men' model is the father who combines being the breadwinner with a presence in the home, often nurturing but also instilling gender-based role modelling on his children. At the opposite end of the continuum is the father who is extensively involved in the care of his child in the 'hands-on' model. Brannen and Nilsen (2006) suggest that whilst the work-focused model has been in evidence over time, it is now much less prevalent than in the past. Whilst the 'family men' model became more common, this is now being surpassed by the 'hands-on' model.

Other terms, such as 'patriarch', 'disciplinarian', 'moral overseer' and the 'new father', can be used to describe the various different models of fatherhood. These labels indicate the primary focus of the roles and responsibilities undertaken by fathers who conform to that particular model. Whilst the predominance of any one particular model has waxed and waned over the past two centuries, it may well be the case that all of these models can still be identified to some extent in families in today's society. In contrast, Masciadrelli et al (2006) suggest that many of the ideas expressed within the various contemporary models of fatherhood are not new but have merely been redefined to reflect fashionable mores, and as a result tend to offer a rather utopian view of fatherhood. Consequently, the varying expectations of society generally and different cultures and individual families more specifically, may lead to conflict for some fathers who find themselves trying to conform to everyone else's expectations in addition to their own.

Whilst external social and economic forces have clearly impacted on the role of the father over time, fathers have in most cases responded proactively to these factors and have embraced the opportunities for their role to evolve.

So what is the role of the father in the UK today? For many fathers, their current roles and responsibilities reflect that of the 'new father' which was first described in the 1980s amongst the middle-classes (Jackson, 1983). This father portrays explicit nurturing behaviours and is more actively involved in his child's care and upbringing than fathers were in the past (Lewis and O'Brien, 1987; Macfadyen et al, 2011). Whilst the overall amount of time they spend with their children has not in many cases changed, fathers have developed ways of using their time more effectively, and interact with their children in more direct ways (Lewis and Warin, 2001). Fathers are now expected to undertake a broader range of responsibilities, many aspects of which were previously the exclusive territory of the mother. As a consequence, the role of today's fathers, whilst having elements in common with their own father's behaviours and attitudes (Brannen and Nilsen, 2006), often differs considerably from them (Barclay and Lupton, 1999; Fägerskiöld, 2008).

It seems, therefore, that the more traditional models of fatherhood are now regarded by most people as being outdated. A father in today's society is expected to support his partner during pregnancy and childbirth, participate in the care of his children from birth onwards and make a greater 'hands-on' contribution to the running of the home. The majority of fathers want this level of involvement and feel comfortable and confident about caring for their children in a more direct way than their own father or grandfather might have done (Thompson et al, 2005; Smeaton and Marsh, 2006).

However, whilst the new father can be observed in many families, in others this is not the case (Lewis and O'Brien, 1987). Some fathers may be selective about the ways in which they contribute to the overall running of the family home, with childcare taking a lower priority. In most families, it is still usually the mother who primarily communicates with healthcare professionals about their child (Macfadyen et al, 2011). In addition, whilst Sullivan (2000) identified that men spent more time caring for their children in 1997 than they did in 1975, the imbalance in time spent by mothers and fathers caring for their children remained the same. Women spent substantially more time caring for their children than their partners, irrespective of whether or not they were in full-time or part-time employment (Hochschild, 1994; Sullivan, 2000). For some fathers these differences may be due to financial constraints, employment, or other external pressures (O'Brien and Shemilt, 2003; Equal Opportunities Commission, 2007). Indeed, fathers may feel guilty that they are not as involved with their children as they would like and worry that they will be labelled by some as being bad or poor fathers as a consequence.

In contrast, some may regard fathers who are actively involved in their child's life, particularly the 'stay-at-home' father as being 'soft' and not conforming with male 'macho' stereotypes. So whilst the 'new father' model may be the ideal for most men and their families, there may be obstacles and threats to be overcome by fathers who would like to adopt this approach. Role conflict, the expectations of themselves and others, and external pressures shape the roles and responsibilities of fathers today. Factors that determine what fathers do and do not do are complex and multifaceted. It is apparent, however, that in many families separate, clearly defined maternal and paternal roles no longer exist (Tiller, 1995).

Reconciling realities

Sadly we do not live in a perfect world. As we will see in subsequent chapters, for some fathers childbirth and the newborn period do not always follow normal or more usual pathways. There are also some situations that have the potential to challenge a father's expectations and experiences of fatherhood. To emphasise some of these challenges, in the following section we examine two examples. The first focuses on fathers who experience depression or mental illness and the second examines the experiences of young fathers. Through our consideration of these two situations we highlight the importance of context (both in relation to temporal and environmental space) and health to the fatherhood experience.

Depression and mental illness

For the majority of fathers, pregnancy, childbirth and early parenthood are positive experiences, albeit that these landmark events can provoke temporary feelings of anxiety, distress and uncertainty. However, for some men, events occurring around the birth of their child can lead to or exacerbate depression and mental illness (Department of Health, 2009a; Chin et al, 2011). About 4% of fathers experience depression during their child's first year, with a peak incidence between 3 and 6 months after the birth (Davé et al, 2010; Paulson and Bazemore, 2010). Fathers are also primarily placed to cushion the effect of their partner's mental health problems (Cuthbert et al, 2011).

Following years of extensive research, there is now an established body of evidence regarding the incidence and risk factors associated with maternal post-natal depression and post-traumatic stress disorder (PTSD) following childbirth

(Creedy et al, 2000; Soet et al, 2003, Ingram and Taylor, 2007; Redshaw and van den Akker, 2007). This is not the case for paternal perinatal depression, although this is now increasingly being investigated (Eriksson et al, 2006; Parfitt and Ayers, 2009; Letourneau et al, 2012). Indeed, recent evidence suggests that depression is more common in new fathers than in the general population of men (Paulson et al, 2009). However, little is known about fathers' experiences of PTSD following childbirth.

An extensive and comprehensive literature review by Bradley and Slade (2011) suggests that up to one third of new fathers may experience symptoms of depression around the time of the birth of their baby. This should be a cause for concern for providers of health and social care (Paulson and Bazemore, 2010). The mental health problems experienced by new fathers can range from anxiety and depression to PTSD and psychosis. A vast array of associated factors have been suggested, including the father's personal experiences of being parented, low relationship satisfaction, social and demographic factors, a history of depression, being younger, and a negative experience of the birth and immediate care of the baby (Davé et al, 2010; Harvey, 2010; Bradley and Slade, 2011). Some studies have also shown a correlation between the incidence of maternal and paternal depression (Buist et al, 2003; Paulson and Bazemore, 2010; Bradley and Slade, 2011). However, it is difficult to determine whether this is a causal relationship (Bradley and Slade, 2011). Maternal and paternal postpartum depression may also manifest itself in different ways.

The potential impact of paternal depression on children has also been noted. Fathers with depression are more likely to display negative parenting behaviours (Buist et al, 2003; Paulson et al, 2009; Davis et al, 2011). This in turn can have a negative impact on a child's behaviour and psychosocial wellbeing (Ramchandani et al, 2005; Paulson and Bazemore, 2010). Indeed Tryvaud et al (2010) suggest that mental health problems in either parent are associated with greater social and emotional dysregulation in their children, regardless of whether their children are born preterm or at term.

There is conflicting evidence about when during the perinatal period fathers are most at risk of mental health problems. A decade ago, studies indicated that paternal distress was highest during the antenatal period (Buist et al, 2003; Condon et al, 2004), whilst a more recent meta-analysis has shown a higher incidence at three to six months post-partum (Paulson et al, 2009). This inconsistency may reflect the increase in the number of studies of paternal depression in recent years. In addition, fathers may now be more comfortable about reporting their mental health problems. Whilst the body of evidence is slowly growing in relation to paternal perinatal depression (Eriksson et al, 2006; Parfitt and Ayers, 2009) there is still much work to be done in this area, particularly in relation to the underlying causes and risk factors and the most appropriate support strategies (Paulson and Bazemore, 2010; Letourneau et al, 2012).

The incidence of paternal depression may be higher than is reported because the attention of healthcare professionals tends to focus on the mother and the baby (Buist et al, 2003). There is therefore a need for greater awareness amongst healthcare professionals regarding paternal perinatal depression and more extensive screening of paternal mental health during the perinatal period (Paulson and Bazemore, 2010).

Young fathers

At what age is a father deemed to be a 'young' father? Whilst there is no universally accepted consensus on this, it is generally deemed to be when a father is under 18 years of age. However, it is perhaps worth considering whether the definition should be less about chronological age and more about level of maturity and preparedness for fatherhood and its subsequent responsibilities. Nevertheless, the literature pertaining to young fatherhood to date generally focuses on chronological age. Within this literature, a number of inter-related factors and risks associated with young fatherhood have been documented (Wilkes et al, 2012). These include lower socio-economic groups, financial hardship, exclusion, history of youth offences, minimum level of education, frequent changes of address, a chaotic pattern of school attendance and multi-parenting (Tyrer et al, 2005; Benjamin and Furstenberg, 2007; Reeves, 2008).

Recent research has begun to challenge some of these negative stereotypes (Tuffin et al, 2010); just because some or all of these factors apply to a particular 'young' father, does not automatically make him a 'poor' father. Indeed, rather than absolving themselves of any involvement or responsibility for their child, many young fathers would like to play a significant role in their child's life (Webb, 2008; Wilkes et al, 2012). Healthcare professionals should therefore be careful not to make hasty and potentially inaccurate judgements about young fathers. However, such fathers often feel as though they are being judged by healthcare professionals (Department of Health, 2010). They can also face discouragement by the poor organisation of these services and, in more extreme cases, opposition from family and friends such that they feel marginalised or excluded. The mother's family may act as gate-keeper and the maternal grandmother often has a strong influence on the nature and extent of the father's involvement (Gavin et al, 2002). The father's family and friends may also discourage involvement of a father with his child, and peer pressure can be very persuasive at this time (Corlyon and McGuire 1997; Reeves and Rehal, 2008).

The role uncertainty and conflicting emotions felt by any man who is about to become a father, can be more extreme for young fathers (Buist et al, 2003; Wilkes et al, 2012), who may have had a poor experience of being fathered themselves (St John et al, 2005; Tyrer et al, 2005). However, fatherhood can be a positive experience for young fathers. It may stimulate a turning point in their life as they form an emotional connection with their child. They may also relish the responsibilities and maturity that fatherhood affords them (Foster, 2004), viewing it as a potentially transformative experience (Letherby et al, 2004). For some young men, fatherhood enables them to establish a family of their own for the first time (Tyrer et al, 2005). It is also important to note that young fatherhood can be controversial and is more acceptable in some cultures than in others.

Pregnancy, childbirth and early parenthood provide ideal opportunities to capture a father's attention, and fathers who are involved during pregnancy are more likely to maintain their involvement after the birth (Burgess, 2008). Although the drive to engage and involve fathers in the UK over recent years has included initiatives that focus on young fathers (National Audit Office, 2006; Department of Health, 2009b), they are still less likely to attend antenatal appointments and parentcraft sessions (Royal College of Midwives, 2012). In addition, they often feel unwelcome when they do attend (Department of Health, 2010). Healthcare professionals delivering maternity and early childhood care therefore have an important role to play in acknowledging, engaging and involving young fathers (Gale, 2008).

Conclusion

Within this chapter, we have seen that making the transition to fatherhood and forming an emotional connection with the child is not always a straightforward process. Despite the fundamental effects on a man's life of becoming a father, much of the process in this transition is taken for granted and implicit. A number of factors can impact upon these processes, many of which can be beyond the control of the father himself. There are increasing external pressures and expectations placed upon men to be 'good' fathers. Whilst most men want to be actively involved and engaged with their children, healthcare professionals need to look to ways of facilitating this process, particularly during the perinatal period.

Key points

- A man's transition to fatherhood can be a challenging, multifaceted and individual formative process
- Fathers are generally under-represented in the parent–infant attachment literature
- A number of internal and external factors can influence the emotional connection that a father forms with his child
- Varying models of fatherhood have been described. Whilst differences still exist, men are generally more actively involved in their child's life than their own father or grandfathers
- Factors such as depression, mental illness and young fatherhood can alter a father's expectations and experiences of fatherhood.

Case history 1
Coping with transition to fatherhood

Paul's partner Tiffany is 32 weeks pregnant. This is their first child. They had been trying to conceive for some time. Tiffany intends to take her full maternity leave entitlement when the baby arrives. She has decorated the nursery and has been buying clothes and equipment for the baby. Paul has been working as much overtime as he can in an attempt to ease the impact of this expenditure. Paul thinks that he should be excited about his child's imminent arrival but instead feels tired, worried and overwhelmed. He feels guilty about feeling this way. He is also having difficulty sleeping. He has not discussed these feelings with anyone and does not want to upset Tiffany.

Reflective questions

- What factors may be causing Paul to feel this way?
- What might be the short and longer-term impact of Paul's current feelings?
- What resources could Paul access for guidance and support at this time?
- What strategies and interventions could the healthcare team use to support Paul?

**Case history 2
A young father**

Jason is 17 years of age and lives with his mother and two younger brothers, Zak and Alfie. He has a different father than his two brothers. Whilst Zak and Alfie see their father fairly regularly, Jason has not had any contact with his father for over 10 years. Jason's mother currently has several part-time jobs and often leaves Jason in charge of his younger brothers. Jason dreams of being a professional musician and is a student at a local college. However, his college attendance is sporadic as he prefers to spend time with his friends and cousins. Jason's girlfriend, Jasmine, is also 17 years old and she is 20 weeks pregnant. Jasmine's mother dislikes Jason and his family, and is trying to prevent her from having any contact with them. Jason is excited about the baby and would like to be a more effective parent than his own father has been. Jasmine is also excited about the baby and hopes that she and Jason will one day live together with their child. Jason is aware that Jasmine's mother dislikes him. Jason's friends and cousins say he should take Jasmine's mother's attitude as an opportunity to relinquish any responsibilities or involvement with his child.

Reflective questions

* Why may Jasmine's mother be responding in this way?
* What factors could be influencing Jason's feelings towards his child?
* What strategies and interventions could the healthcare team use to facilitate the involvement and engagement of Jason in the pregnancy, birth and subsequent care of his child?

References

Barclay L, Lupton D (1999) The experiences of new fatherhood: A socio-cultural analysis. *Journal of Advanced Nursing* **29**(4): 1013–20

Bateman L, Bharj K (2009) The impact of the birth on the couple's relationship. *Evidence Based Midwifery* **7**(1): 16–23

Benjamin K, Furstenberg F (2007) Multipartnered fertility among young women with a nonmarital first birth. Prevalence and risk factors. *Perspectives on Sexual and Reproductive Health* **39**: 29–38

Billings JR (1995) Bonding theory – tying mothers in knots? A critical review of the application of a theory to nursing. *Journal of Clinical Nursing* **4**: 207–11

Bondas-Salonen T (1998) How women experience the presence of their partners at the births of their babies. *Qualitative Health Research* **8**: 784–800

Boulton MG (1983) *On being a mother.* Tavistock Publications, London

Bowen SM, Miller BC (1980) Paternal attachment behavior as related to presence at delivery and parenthood classes: A pilot study. *Nursing Research* **29**: 307–11

Bowlby J (1988) *A secure base.* Routledge, London

Bowlby J (2005) *The making and breaking of affectional bonds.* Routledge Classics, London

Bradley E, MacKenzie M, Boath E (2004) The experience of first-time fatherhood: A brief report. *Journal of Reproductive and Infant Psychology* **22**(1): 45–7

Bradley R, Slade P (2011) A review of mental health problems in fathers following the birth of a child. *Journal of Reproductive and Infant Psychology* **29**: 19–42

Brannen J, Nilsen A (2006) From fatherhood to fathering: Transmission and change among British fathers in four-generation families. *Sociology* **40**(2): 335–52

Bretherton I (1992) The origins of attachment theory: John Bowlby and Mary Ainsworth. *Developmental Psychology* **28**: 759–75

Bretherton I, Lambert JD, Golby B (2005) Involved fathers of preschool children as seen by themselves and their wives: Accounts of attachment, socialization and companionship. *Attachment and Human Development* **7**: 229–51

Buist A, Morse CA, Durkin S (2003) Men's adjustment to fatherhood: Implications for obstetric health care. *Journal of Obstetric, Gynecologic and Neonatal Nursing* **32**: 172–80

Burgess A (2008) *Maternal and infant health in the perinatal period: The father's role.* The Fatherhood Institute, Abergavenny

Chin R, Hall P, Daiches A (2011) Fathers' experiences of their transition to fatherhood: A metasynthesis. *Journal of Reproductive and Infant Psychology* **29**(1): 4–18

Condon J (2006) What about dad? Psychosocial and mental health issues for new fathers. *Australian Family Physician* **35**: 690–2

Condon JT, Boyce P, Corkindale CJ (2004) The first-time fathers study: A prospective study of the mental health and well-being of men during the transition to parenthood. *Australian and New Zealand Journal of Psychiatry* **38**(1): 56–64

Condon JT, Corkindale CJ, Boyce P (2008) Assessment of postnatal paternal–infant attachment: Development of a questionnaire instrument. *Journal of Reproductive and Infant Psychology* **26**: 195–210

Corlyon J, McGuire C (1997) *Young persons in public care.* National Children's Bureau, London

Creedy DK, Shochet IM, Horsfall J (2000) Childbirth and the development of acute trauma symptoms: Incidence and contributing factors. *Birth* **27**: 104–11

Cuthbert C, Rayns G, Stanley K (2011) *All babies count: Prevention and protection of vulnerable babies.* NSPCC, London

Dartnell L, Ganguly N, Batterham J (2005) *Access to maternity services research report.* Department of Health, London

Davé S, Petersen I, Sherr L, Nazareth I (2010) Incidence of maternal and paternal depression in primary care. *Archives of Pediatric and Adolescent Medicine* **164**: 1038–44

Davis RN, Davis MM, Freed GL, Clark SJ (2011) Father's depression related to positive and negative parenting behaviors with 1-year-old children. *Pediatrics* **127**: 612–18

Deave T, Johnson D (2008) The transition to parenthood: What does it mean for fathers? *Journal of Advanced Nursing* **63**: 626–33

Department of Health (2009a) *Perinatal positive practice guide. Improving access to psychological therapies.* Department of Health, London

Department of Health (2009b) *The family nurse partnership.* Available from: http:www. dh.gov.uk/en/Publications andstatistics/Lettersandcirculars/Dearcolleagueletters/ DH_109448 (accessed 1 March 2012)

Department of Health (2010) *Maternity and early years: Making a good start to family life.* Department of Health, London

Direct Gov UK (2011) *Ordinary paternity leave.* Available from: http://www.direct.gov. uk/en/index.htm (accessed 6 September 2011)

Draper J (2002a) 'It's the first scientific evidence': men's experience of pregnancy confirmation. *Journal of Advanced Nursing* **39**: 563–570

Draper J (2002b) 'It was a real good show': The ultrasound scan, fathers and the power of visual knowledge. *Sociology of Health and Illness* **24**: 771–95

Draper J (2003) Men's passage to fatherhood: An analysis of the contemporary relevance of transition theory. *Nursing Inquiry* **10**: 66–78

Equal Opportunities Commission (2007) *The state of the modern family.* Equal Opportunities Commission, Manchester

Eriksson C, Westman G, Hamberg K (2006) Content of childbirth-related fear in Swedish women and men – analysis of an open-ended question. *Journal of Midwifery and Women's Health* **51**: 112–18

Fagan J, Bernd E, Whiteman V (2007) Adolescent fathers' parenting stress, social support and involvement with infants. *Journal of Research on Adolescents* **17**: 1–22

Fägerskiöld A (2008) A change in life as experienced by first-time fathers. *Scandinavian Journal of Caring Science* **22**: 64–71

Field T (2007) *The amazing infant.* Blackwell Publishing, Oxford

Flacking R, Ewald U, Hedberg Nyqvist K, Starrin B (2006) Trustful bonds: A key to 'becoming a mother' and to reciprocal breastfeeding. Stories of mothers of very preterm infants at a neonatal unit. *Social Science and Medicine* **62**(1): 70–80

Foster J (2004) Fatherhood and the meaning of children: An ethnographic study among Puerto Rican partners of adolescent mothers. *Journal of Midwifery and Women's Health* **49**: 118–25

Gale L (2008) A father is born. In: Reeves J (ed) *Inter-professional approaches to young fathers*. M&K Update Ltd, Keswick

Gavin LE, Black MM, Minor S, Abel Y, Papas M, Bentley M (2002) Young disadvantaged fathers involvement with their infants. *Journal of Adolescent Health* **31**: 266–76

Genesoni L, Tallandini MA (2009) Men's psychological transition to fatherhood: Analysis of the literature, 1989–2008. *Birth* **36**(4): 305–17

Harvey ME (2010) *The experiences and perceptions of fathers attending the birth and immediate care of their baby*. Unpublished PhD Thesis. Aston University, Birmingham

Henderson AD, Brouse AJ (1991) The experiences of new fathers during the first 3 weeks of life. *Journal of Advanced Nursing* **16**(3): 293–8

Henwood K, Procter J (2003) The 'good father': Reading men's accounts of paternal involvement during the transition to first-time fatherhood. *British Journal of Social Psychology* **42**(3): 337–55

Hjelmstedt A, Widsröm A-M, Collins A (2007) Prenatal attachment in Swedish IVF fathers and controls. *Journal of Reproductive and Infant Psychology* **25**: 296–307

Hochschild AR (1994) The second shift: Employed women are putting in another day of work at home. In: Kimmel MS, Messner MA (eds) *Men's lives* (3rd edn). Allyn and Bacon, Needham Heights MA

Hugill K (2009) *The experiences and emotion work of fathers in a neonatal unit*. Unpublished PhD thesis. University of Central Lancashire, Preston

Ingram J, Taylor J (2007) Predictors of postnatal depression: Using antenatal needs assessment discussion tool. *Journal of Reproductive and Infant Psychology* **25**: 210–22

Jackson B (1983) *Fatherhood*. George Allen & Unwin, London

Jackson K, Ternestedt B-M, Schollin J (2003) From alienation to familiarity: Experiences of mothers and fathers of preterm babies. *Journal of Advanced Nursing* **43**: 120–9

Klaus MH, Jerauld R, Kreger NC, McAlpine W, Steffa M, Kennell JH (1972) Maternal attachment: Importance of the first post-partum days. *New England Journal of Medicine* **286**: 460–3

Klaus MH, Kennell JH (1982) *Parent–infant bonding* (2nd edn). CV Mosby, St. Louis MO

Lamb M (1997) The development of the father relationship. In: Lamb M (ed) *The role of the father in child development* (3rd edn). Wiley, New York NY

Letherby G, Brady G, Butler G (2004) *Experiences and support needs of 'young' fathers in Warwickshire*. Centre for Social Justice Coventry University, Coventry

Letourneau N, Tryphonopoulos PD, Duffett-Leger L, et al (2012) Support intervention needs and preferences of fathers affected by postpartum depression. *Journal of Perinatal and Neonatal Nursing* **26**: 69–80

Lewis C, O'Brien M (1987) What good are dads? *Father Facts* **1**: 1–12

Lewis C, Warin J (2001) Constraints on fathers: Research, history and clinical practice. In: Lewis C, O'Brien M (eds) *Reassessing fatherhood*. Sage Publications, London

Locock L, Alexander J (2006) 'Just a bystander'? Men's place in the process of fetal screening and diagnosis. *Social Science and Medicine* **62**: 1349–59

Lundqvist P, Jakobsson L (2003) Swedish men's experiences of becoming fathers to their preterm infants. *Neonatal Network* **22**(6): 25–31

McCreight BS (2004) A grief ignored: Narratives of pregnancy loss from a male perspective. *Sociology of Health and Illness* **26**: 326–50

McElliot M (2001) Antenatal information wanted by first time fathers. *British Journal of Midwifery* **9**: 556–8

McFadyen A (1994) *Special care babies and their developing relationships*. Routledge, London

Macfadyen A, Swallow V, Santacroce S, Lambert H (2011) Involving fathers in research. *Journal for Specialists in Pediatric Nursing* **16**: 216–19

McVeigh CA, Baafi M, Williamson M (2002) Functional status after fatherhood: An Australian study. *Journal of Obstetric, Gynaecologic and Neonatal Nursing* **31**: 165–71

Masciadrelli BP, Pleck JH, Stueve JL (2006) Fathers' role model perceptions. *Men and Masculinities* **9**(23): 23–34

Meadows S (1986) *Understanding child development*. Unwin Hyman, London

Mercer RT, Ferketich SL (1990) Predictors of parental attachment during early parenthood. *Journal of Advanced Nursing* **15**: 268–80

Mottram L (2008) First-time expectant fathers and their influence on decision making regarding choice for place of birth. *MIDIRS Midwifery Digest* **18**: 582–9

National Audit Office (2006) *Sure Start children centres*. The Stationery Office, London

O'Brien M, Shemilt I (2003) *Working fathers: Earning and Caring Research Discussion Series*. Equal Opportunities Commission, Manchester

Parfitt YM, Ayers S (2009) The effect of post-natal symptoms of post-traumatic stress and depression on the couple's relationship and parent–baby bond. *Journal of Reproductive and Infant Psychology* **27**: 127–42

Paulson JF, Bazemore SD (2010) Prenatal and postpartum depression in fathers and its association with maternal depression: A meta-analysis. *Journal of the American Medical Association* **303**: 1961–9

Paulson JF, Keefe HA, Leiferman JA (2009) Early parental depression and child language development. *Journal of Child Psychology and Psychiatry* **50**: 254–62

Premberg A, Hellström A, Berg M (2008) Experiences of the first year as a father. *Scandinavian Journal of Caring Science* **22**: 56–63

Puddifoot JE, Johnson MP (1999) Active grief, despair and difficulty coping: Some measured characteristics of male response following their partner's miscarriage. *Journal of Reproductive and Infant Psychology* **17**: 89–93

Ramchandani P, Stein A, Evans J, O'Connor TG, and the ALSPAC study team (2005) Paternal depression in the postnatal period and child development: A prospective population study. *Lancet* **365**: 2201–5

Redshaw ME, Rowe R, Hockley C Brocklehurst P (2007) *Recorded delivery: A national survey of women's experience of maternity care 2006.* National Perinatal Epidemiology Unit, Oxford

Redshaw M, van den Akker O (2007) Maternal health and wellbeing. *Journal of Reproductive and Infant Psychology* **25**: 253–4

Reeves J (2006) Recklessness, rescue and responsibility: Young men tell their stories of the transition to fatherhood. *Practice* **18**(2): 79–90

Reeves J (2008) Introduction. In: Reeves J (ed) *Inter-professional approaches to young fathers.* M&K Update Ltd, Keswick

Reeves J, Rehal F (2008) Contextualising the evidence: Young fathers, family and professional support. In: Reeves J (ed) *Inter-professional approaches to young fathers.* M&K Update Ltd, Keswick

Richards MPM (1983) Parent–child relationships: Some general considerations. In: Davis JA, Richards MPM, Roberton NRC (eds) *Parent baby attachment in premature infants.* Croom Helm, Beckenham

Riikka Korjaa R, Maunuc J, Kirjavainene J et al (2008) Mother–infant interaction is influenced by the amount of holding in preterm infants. *Early Human Development* **84**: 257–67

Roeber J (1987) *Shared parenthood.* Century Hutchinson Ltd, London

Royal College of Midwives (2012) *Reaching out: Involving fathers in maternity care.* Royal College of Midwives, London

St John W, Cameron C, McVeigh C (2005) Meeting the challenges of new fatherhood during the early weeks. *Journal of Obstetric, Gynecologic and Neonatal Nursing* **34**: 80–189

Singh D, Newburn M (2000) *Becoming a father: Men's access to information and support about pregnancy, birth and life with a new baby.* National Childbirth Trust and Fathers Direct, London

Smeaton D, Marsh A (2006) *Maternity and paternity rights and benefits: Survey of parents 2005.* Department of Trade and Industry, London

Smith JA (1999) Identity development during the transition to motherhood: An interpretive phenomenological analysis. *Journal of Reproductive and Infant Psychology* **17**(3): 281–99

Smith N (1998) Antenatal classes and the transition to fatherhood: A study of some father's views. *MIDIRS Midwifery Digest* **9**: 463–8

Soet JE, Brack GA, Dilorio C (2003) Prevalence and predictors of women's experience of psychological trauma during childbirth. *Birth* **30**: 36–46

Sullivan JR (1999) Development of father–infant attachment in fathers of preterm infants. *Neonatal Network* **18**(7): 33–9

Sullivan O (2000) The division of domestic labour. *Sociology* **34**: 437–56

Thompson M, Vinter L, Young V (2005) *Dads and their babies: Leave arrangements in the first year. Working Paper Series No. 37*. Equal Opportunities Commission, Manchester

Tiller CM (1995) Fathers' parenting attitudes during a child's first year. *Journal of Obstetric Gynecologic and Neonatal Nursing* **24**: 508–14

Tryvaud K, Anderson VA, Lee KJ, Woodward LJ, et al (2010) Parental mental health and early social–emotional development of children born very preterm. *Journal of Pediatric Psychology* **35**(7): 768–77

Tuffin K, Rouch G, Frewin K (2010) Constructing adolescent fatherhood: Responsibilities and intergenerational repair. *Culture, Health and Society* **12**(5): 485–98

Turton P, Badenhorst W, Hughes P, Ward J, Riches S, White S (2006) Psychological impact of stillbirth on fathers in the subsequent pregnancy and puerperium. *British Journal of Psychiatry* **188**: 165–72

Tyrer P, Chase E, Warwick I, Aggleton P (2005) 'Dealing with it' Experiences of young fathers in and leaving care. *British Journal of Social Work* **35**: 1107–21

Webb J (2008) The legislative and policy context of young fathers and their children. In: Reeves J (ed) *Inter-professional approaches to young fathers*. M&K Update Ltd, Keswick

White MA, Wilson ME, Elander G, Persson B (1999) The Swedish family: Transitions to parenthood. *Scandinavian Journal of Caring Sciences* **13**: 171–6

Wilkes L, Mannix J, Jackson D (2012) 'I am going to be a dad': Experiences and expectations of adolescent and young adult expectant fathers. *Journal of Clinical Nursing* **21**(1–2): 180–8

World Health Organization (2007) *Fatherhood and health outcomes in Europe*. World Health Organization, Copenhagen

Chapter 4

Fathers at the birth

Merryl Harvey

Introduction

Childbirth is the landmark event in a man's transition to fatherhood. Indeed many fathers have described their child's birth as being a life-changing experience. This chapter explores the changing trends in the presence and involvement of fathers in childbirth in the UK over the past 50 years. Evidence regarding fathers' experiences of normal, complicated and preterm childbirth and situations where the baby requires resuscitation at delivery will also be explored. Strategies that could be used to engage and involve fathers more readily during childbirth will then be suggested. The chapter ends with two case histories to facilitate reflection on ways in which fathers can be supported during and immediately following childbirth.

Although a prospective father may try to prepare both practically and emotionally for fatherhood during the pregnancy, the child can often seem unreal before the birth (Draper, 1997). It is the birth of his child that signifies to himself and others that he is now a father. From this moment on, whatever his subsequent relationship with his child, he will always be a father. For many fathers, seeing their baby at the delivery or shortly afterwards is the most important factor in forming an emotional connection with his child. Childbirth can often therefore be an emotional time for a new father, irrespective of whether or not he is present at the delivery itself.

Most fathers in the UK are present at their child's birth, although the exact number is unclear. This is because some studies combine data regarding presence during labour and during birth (Singh and Newburn, 2003). Other reports do not define the term 'birth partner', so the data may include other relatives or friends who were present at the birth and not just the father (Redshaw et al, 2007). Taking these factors into consideration, around 87–97% of fathers attend the birth of their baby in the UK in the 21st century (Early, 2001; Kiernan and Smith, 2003; TNS System Three, 2005). However, in recent times, fathers do more than just attend the birth; in most cases they are also now expected to participate in their partner's care and interact as soon as possible with their baby (Chan and Paterson-Brown, 2002; Castle et al, 2008). Whilst this has brought a further dimension to a father's experience of childbirth, the literature on fathers' perceptions of this level of involvement is limited. Early reports of fathers' experiences often relied on proxy accounts that were given by mothers or healthcare professionals (Bondas-Salonen, 1998), whilst other studies have focused on his role, rather than the impact on him of the birth (Chalmers and Meyer, 1996; Johnson, 2002). This chapter endeavours to redress this imbalance.

Fathers attending delivery: Historical overview

For many centuries in the UK, supporting mothers during labour and assisting with childbirth was almost exclusively the domain of women and male obstetricians. Fathers were rarely involved in a direct way (Draper, 1997). As a consequence, the exclusion of fathers became self-perpetuating because, with no specific role to play during childbirth, there were no other reasons why a father should attend his child's birth (Bedford and Johnson, 1988). The possible benefits of the father's presence, either to himself or others, were not considered. Consequently, the generally held view was that the remote father figure that was prevalent during most 19th and 20th century families was also evident during pregnancy and childbirth (Burgess, 1997). However, it is likely that more fathers attended and participated in childbirth during this period than has previously been acknowledged (Foyster, 1999; Francis, 2002). Most births during this time occurred at home and it is not known how many fathers did in fact attend the delivery, because this information was not usually recorded (Burgess, 1997).

By the 1950s the balance was beginning to shift away from home births with an increase in the number taking place in hospitals or nursing homes (Donnison, 1988; Shribman, 2007). When childbirth took place in these settings, the father was usually barred from the delivery room and was often sent home or to separate waiting rooms (so-called 'stork clubs' – Leavitt, 2003) to await the birth (Bedford and Johnson, 1988; Draper, 2003). During the 1960s and 1970s the move away from birth at home, under the auspices of the midwife, to being a more medicalised event in hospital under the control of mostly male obstetricians continued (Draper, 1997). This trend accelerated in the 1980s with the view that all mothers should give birth in hospital (Shribman, 2007). As childbirth became more medicalised, mothers increasingly felt they needed an advocate during childbirth in hospital. Fathers began to take on this role (Odent, 1999) and from this time onwards, an increasing number of men attended the birth of their baby (Early, 2001; World Health Organization, 2007). However, many hospitals imposed sanctions and conditions before this was allowed. For example, fathers were usually required to have previously attended parentcraft classes (Cronenwett and Newmark, 1974) and it was made clear that the sole reason for a father's attendance was to support his partner rather than for any personal benefit to himself (Burgess, 1997).

Support for the presence of fathers during childbirth during the 1980s was not unanimous (Draper, 1997). Many in the medical profession expressed concern that fathers would be distracting and disruptive and that this would impact on healthcare professionals' ability to undertake their responsibilities (Leavitt, 2003). Some also argued that letting fathers into the birth room would lead to an increased risk of litigation (Brown, 1982; Chapman, 1992). It was also believed that the presence of the father would increase the incidence of infection and compromise the couple's future relationship (Cronenwett and Newmark, 1974; Bedford and Johnson, 1988; Early, 2001). There was also the view that it was 'unnatural' for a father to want to be present during his child's birth (Burgess, 1997). Some also ally the medicalisation of childbirth to its deliberate mystification by obstetricians to ensure they retained control over the process (Draper, 1997; Early, 2001).

Nevertheless, by the late 1980s, most fathers attended their child's birth (Jacoby, 1987). Over the past two decades, the short and longer-term benefits of the father's presence during childbirth have been increasingly recognised. This recognition is reflected in the drive to engage and involve fathers more readily during pregnancy, childbirth and the postnatal period (Department of Health and Department for Education and Skills, 2004; National Institute for Health and Clinical Excellence, 2006; Shribman, 2007). Today, fathers are expected not only to be present during the birth but also to support their partner during labour, participate in her care and interact with the baby as soon as possible after delivery (Chan and Paterson-Brown, 2002; Castle et al, 2008; Kunjappy-Clifton, 2008). A father's presence and involvement during childbirth has therefore become a key feature of the 'new father' role.

Fathers encountering normal childbirth

Most of the research exploring men's experiences of childbirth has, to date, focused on the fathers of healthy babies who were born at term by normal delivery (Morse et al, 2000; Condon et al, 2004; Montigny and Lacharité, 2004). When reviewing the literature it is evident that definitions of 'normal' childbirth vary, particularly in international literature. To accommodate these variations, in the following section, a normal delivery is defined as being a vaginal birth without the aid of instruments. When the literature is reviewed, three key themes are apparent: 'the impact on the father', 'the father's role' and 'the impact of the father's presence on others'.

Impact on the father

Childbirth can be a positive experience for fathers (Chalmers and Meyer, 1996; Somers-Smith, 1999; Kunjappy-Clifton, 2008), although the precise reasons for this are not clearly established (Mander, 2004). Nevertheless, fathers have described childbirth as being an enriching, joyous, euphoric and life-affirming experience (Chandler and Field, 1997; Vehviläinen-Julkunen and Liukkonen, 1998; Premberg et al, 2011). Relief that the baby and their partner are well enhances their joy (Chandler and Field, 1997). Fathers are also often in awe of their partner's endurance and capacity to cope with the pain of childbirth (Fägerskiöld, 2008; Harvey, 2010). Many fathers see attending the birth of their child as being a rite of passage and the most important stage in their transition to fatherhood (Jackson, 1983; Bedford and Johnson, 1988; Draper, 1997; Longworth and Kingdon, 2011). Witnessing the birth may also be an important factor in confirming their identity as a parent and their concomitant new roles and responsibilities, and facilitating father–infant attachment (Klaus and Kennell, 1982; World Health Organization, 2007). Fathers derive satisfaction from feeling they have been helpful to their partner (Berry, 1988; Somers-Smith, 1999; Rosich-Medina and Shetty, 2007) and often describe attending the birth as being a turning point in their life (Burgess, 1997).

However, fathers can also experience a number of negative feelings when present during normal childbirth. Some feel pressurised into taking on an active role (Chapman, 1992; Harvey, 2010). They can also feel helpless and useless and find it difficult seeing their partner in pain (Vehviläinen-Julkunen and Liukkonen, 1998; Somers-Smith, 1999; Kunjappy-Clifton, 2008). Fathers become more anxious as labour progresses, with the delivery being the most stressful part of their childbirth experience (Berry, 1988; Johnson, 2002). This has been described as a father's 'personal Everest' (Jackson, 1983: 69). As the delivery approaches, their focus of concern usually changes from their partner to the baby (Chandler and Field, 1997). Fathers dread the actual birth and worry that the baby will not survive (Eriksson et al, 2006).

Fathers experience difficulty coping with the uncertainty of childbirth even when labour and delivery are straightforward (Kunjappy-Clifton, 2008). They often report feeling marginalised, excluded and abandoned (Chandler and Field, 1997; Early, 2001; Draper, 2003). The authors of a qualitative study involving eight fathers described them as being a 'shocked bystander' (Dartnell et al, 2005: 58). In many instances this isolation is compounded by feeling they have no control over what is happening (Draper, 2003; Rosich-Medina and Shetty, 2007;

Harvey, 2010). For many men this lack of control can be a unique experience, as they may feel they have control over all other aspects of their life. Sometimes fathers become increasingly more questioning, challenging or agitated and, in more extreme cases, aggressive, as the delivery approaches. This may also be because they feel they do not have any control over what is happening and they feel excluded (Harvey, 2010).

Fathers who experience negative emotions during childbirth often endeavour to control these feelings in order to protect their partner (Chandler and Field, 1997; Somers-Smith, 1999). This response may be compounded by their perception that to display negative emotions would be a sign of weakness (Sullivan-Lyons, 1998; Harvey, 2010). Consequently, some fathers find it difficult to support their partner when trying to cope with their own emotions (Berry, 1988; Enkin et al, 2000; Kunjappy-Clifton, 2008). They may also distance themselves from what is happening or use distraction strategies as a way of controlling their emotions (Harvey, 2012). In a few more extreme cases, fathers are traumatised by normal birth and some require support afterwards (Burgess, 1997; White, 2007; Kunjappy-Clifton, 2008). A number of factors, such as a father's underlying fear of hospitals, could impinge upon his childbirth experiences in this setting (Burgess, 1997).

So whilst fathers do report positive experiences of normal childbirth, the literature often reports a more negative view. However, it should be recognised that this could be the result of methodological limitations. For example, studies sometimes involve small samples (Chapman, 1992), have limited variability within the sample (Kunjappy-Clifton, 2008), and only involve self-selecting participants (Draper, 2003). Nevertheless, it would appear that even normal childbirth can be an experience that fathers find both difficult and challenging.

The father's role

The most commonly cited role that fathers undertake during normal childbirth is to support their partner (Klein et al, 1981; Berry, 1988; Morse et al, 2000). More specifically, fathers provide emotional support, physical contact and direct care. The latter often includes providing drinks and massage, helping his partner change her position and assisting with her personal hygiene. It may also include less pleasant tasks, such as holding vomit bowls. Fathers also advocate for their partner and liaise with healthcare professionals (Klein et al, 1981; Bondas-Salonen, 1998; Gungor and Beji, 2007). In some cases they fill in what would otherwise be gaps in her care (Enkin et al, 2000).

Fathers are often best placed to support their partner in these ways because in many cases they are the only constant person throughout the labour and delivery (Bondas-Salonen, 1998). Fathers also usually know the mother better than any other person present at the birth (Longworth, 2006). However, many fathers say after the delivery that they were uncertain what their role was at the time (Sullivan-Lyons, 1998; Kunjappy-Clifton, 2008). Indeed their role is sometimes more clearly defined by what they cannot do than by what they can do (Draper, 1997; Harvey, 2010). This uncertainty and dissonance regarding their role may impact on a father's experiences of childbirth in a negative way.

The expectation that fathers will undertake supportive activities is reflected in the content of parentcraft classes, the main focus of which in relation to fathers is usually how they can best support their partner (Hildingsson and Häggström, 1999; Mander, 2004). This may be a deliberate strategy to reinforce their responsibilities (World Health Organization, 2007). Although many fathers in the UK do not attend parenting classes (Redshaw et al, 2007), those that do will be made aware of the expectation of healthcare professionals and the service more generally, that they will support their partner during labour and the birth.

Frameworks have been developed to describe the different roles fathers adopt during childbirth (Berry, 1988; Chapman, 1992). In a study carried out in the United States involving 20 couples, three possible roles were described: the 'coach' who leads and directs, the 'team-mate' who assists and supports, and the 'witness' who takes on a more distant and passive role (Chapman, 1992). Two decades ago, the most commonly identified role was that of witness (Chapman, 1992), which relates to the era in which the study was undertaken. Despite the small number of participants involved, the setting, and the date of the study, this model has been used in other international childbirth research (Johnson, 2002; Gungor and Beji, 2007; Kunjappy-Clifton, 2008). More recent studies have identified that fathers usually now adopt the more active roles of coach or team-mate (Johnson, 2002; Gungor and Beji, 2007). This reflects not only the greater expectation that fathers now play a more active role during childbirth but also perhaps their increasing desire to do so.

Impact of father's presence on others

Whilst claims have been made about the positive impact on others when fathers are present during childbirth, benefits have not been conclusively shown. It has been reported that the presence of a father shortens labour, reduces the need for operative delivery, reduces the mother's need for analgesia and has a positive impact on a mother's perception of the birth (Berry, 1988; Somers-Smith, 1999; Gungor and Beji, 2007). However, supporting evidence for these claims is rarely provided and it has been suggested that such studies are unsound (Early, 2001). Furthermore, a systematic review of 21 trials identified that the continuous presence of a support person (healthcare professional or lay person) had a positive impact on outcomes (Hodnett et al, 2011). Thus, it appears that the continuous support of anyone, not necessarily the father specifically, is beneficial. Indeed, some have questioned whether a father's presence is advantageous.

It has been claimed that a father may influence the progress of labour in a negative way and damage the couple's long-term relationship, but no evidence for these claims has been provided (Odent, 1999; Longworth, 2006; O'Malley, 2009). Although Odent (2008) argues that the father's presence induces the release of maternal adrenaline, which slows oxytocin activity, this claim is not substantiated and has been challenged by others (O'Malley, 2009). Whatever the case, the risks associated with the presence of fathers previously cited by opponents in the 1980s, such as the increased incidence of infection, appear to be unfounded (Bedford and Johnson, 1988; Chapman, 1992; Mander, 2004). It would seem that there is scope for much more extensive research in this area.

Fathers encountering complicated and preterm childbirth

Whilst for the majority of fathers childbirth is normal and straightforward, for others it is not. The incidence of both complicated childbirth and preterm birth are increasing within the UK and internationally. This rise is primarily as a consequence of developments in reproductive technology and in obstetric and neonatal care (Murphy et al, 2003; Langhoff-Roos et al, 2006). In this context, complicated childbirth is defined as being vaginal instrumental delivery and lower segment caesarean section (LSCS). Preterm birth is defined as being the delivery of a baby (normal or complicated birth) before 37 completed weeks' gestation. The increased incidence of these types of birth (Murphy et al, 2004; Langhoff-Roos et al, 2006) has led to differences in the healthcare professional conducting the delivery, with an increase in deliveries undertaken by doctors (23.7% in 1989–1990 to 35.5% in 2005–2006) and an associated fall in midwife-conducted deliveries (75.6% in 1989–1990 to 64% in 2005–2006) (Healthcare Commission, 2008). As a consequence, for many families childbirth has become a medical event (Shribman, 2007). Although there is an established body of knowledge regarding mothers' experiences of these types of birth (Oakley and Richards, 1990; Simkin, 1992; Ryding et al, 2000), there is limited evidence regarding the impact of these births on fathers (Vehviläinen-Julkunen and Liukkonen, 1998; Johnson, 2002; Parfitt and Ayers, 2009).

Given that most fathers in the UK attend the birth of their baby (Early 2001; TNS System Three, 2005), it can be surmised that more and more fathers are encountering complicated and preterm childbirth. However, little is known about fathers' experiences of these types of birth. This is particularly noteworthy given that on these occasions fathers usually have to deal with more than one significant life event; the birth of their potentially sick and/or preterm baby and their partner undergoing an obstetric intervention (Taylor et al, 2002). Fathers who are present during LSCS also find themselves in an unusual situation, because relatives do not usually attend the surgery of family members.

Complicated and preterm childbirth often involve interventions that are undertaken as an emergency (White, 2007). The birth may occur rapidly, with little prior warning (Calam et al, 1999; White, 2007). These births therefore often involve a high level of uncertainty. The mother may require critical care before and after the delivery (Goebel, 2004; Maternal Critical Care Working Group, 2011) and the baby will almost certainly require ongoing neonatal care if born prematurely or if compromised at birth. In some instances, this may require transfer of the baby to a neonatal unit in another hospital. There may therefore be concern and uncertainty about the mother and the baby's survival, recovery and long-term wellbeing (Jackson et al, 2003; White, 2007). Consequently, some fathers encounter events, the outcome of which is unknown at the time (White, 2007). Indeed, Peterson (2008: 242) has described fathers experiencing these sorts of situations as 'being catapulted into fatherhood'. Whilst the literature regarding fathers' experiences of complicated and preterm childbirth is limited, when reviewed, four key themes can be identified: 'being unprepared', 'emotional impact', 'the father's needs' and 'long-term impact'. There is a correlation between complicated and preterm childbirth, and much of the literature considers these types of birth collectively. Consequently, the findings of the review regarding fathers' experiences of complicated and preterm births are presented together.

Being unprepared

Some fathers who encounter complicated and preterm childbirth will have prior warning that the delivery is imminent. However, in many cases problems arise spontaneously and unexpectedly, leaving little time for preparation (Jackson et al, 2003; Lundqvist and Jakobsson, 2003). Preterm birth, in particular, shortens a father's opportunity to prepare for his transition to fatherhood (Lindberg et al, 2007; Lee et al, 2009). Fathers have described feeling overwhelmed and helpless when they realise their baby would be born early (Lee et al, 2009).

Antenatal preparation may influence whether or not a father feels prepared for preterm or complicated childbirth. Whilst few studies make reference to this, one study investigated the impact of an additional fathers-only session during a course of parentcraft classes which included information about complicated childbirth. Fathers attending the classes were randomised into two groups. Those who accessed the intervention (52) and subsequently encountered complicated childbirth (number not stated) felt they were better prepared and were more able to support their partner than the control group of fathers (48) who did not access the intervention but encountered similar types of delivery (Wöckel et al, 2007). However, antenatal classes usually do not cover complicated and preterm childbirth in any detail, if at all. Fathers also often do not perceive a need to prepare themselves for these types of birth, even when problems are identified during the pregnancy which indicate that an early or complicated delivery is likely to occur. Other fathers who attempt to prepare for these types of birth have reported a lack of appropriate resources (Harvey, 2010).

Emotional impact

Many fathers describe preterm birth as being unreal and frightening (Jackson et al, 2003; Alderson et al, 2006; Lindberg et al, 2007). They also report feelings of denial, anxiety, fear and uncertainty as the delivery gets closer (McCain and Deatrick, 1994; Lundqvist and Jakobsson, 2003). Whilst this is similar to the heightened response that fathers experience as a normal delivery approaches, it is not known if the responses of fathers attending preterm birth are more extreme. Fathers are often shocked at seeing the size of their preterm baby (McCain and Deatrick, 1994; Harvey, 2010) and feel a lack of control over events (Jenni, 2000; Lundqvist and Jakobsson, 2003). Whilst fathers have described being afraid of losing their baby (Lee et al, 2009), men are usually more concerned about their partner when complicated birth occurs (Koppel and Kaiser, 2001; Taylor et al, 2002; Harvey, 2010). This is different to fathers who encounter normal childbirth as their focus of concern usually changes from their partner to the baby as the delivery becomes imminent (Chandler and Field, 1997).

Sometimes, problems affecting the mother or the baby are identified during normal labour, which result in emergency complicated childbirth. Fathers have recalled being frightened when changes in the fetal heart rate were noted (Chandler and Field, 1997; Jenni, 2000; Harvey, 2010). One father who was also a doctor described his distress, 'My own heart seemed to have stopped beating for a moment. I was emotionally distressed as never before' (Jenni, 2000: 139). However, these negative experiences are juxtaposed with the positive feelings fathers experience at their baby's birth. This dichotomy is even more extreme if it was feared that the baby would not survive. Fathers therefore often encounter a joyful experience that is shaded by anxiety and uncertainty (Nolan, 1996; Lundqvist and Jakobsson, 2003).

The evidence regarding fathers' experiences of different types of delivery is conflicting. One survey found that fathers were more anxious during LSCS than other types of delivery and reported that complicated childbirth was less rewarding for fathers because they felt they had been less helpful to their partner (Chan and Paterson-Brown, 2002). Fathers attending LSCS deliveries have also described their baby in less positive ways than those attending normal births (Greenhalgh et al, 2000). Another study reported that fathers attending emergency complicated deliveries felt frustrated and helpless and more anxious than fathers who were present during normal deliveries, although this did not reach statistical significance (Rosich-Medina and Shetty, 2007). Elective complicated childbirth also appears to cause paternal anxiety. In a survey of 91 birth partners, nearly half (42%) had attended a previous LSCS but were just as anxious as first-time birth partners (Taylor et al, 2002). The authors suggest an anxious partner may be less able to support the mother (Taylor et al, 2002). Others have endorsed this view by stating that high paternal anxiety correlates with mothers' negative experiences of LSCS (Keogh et al, 2005). However, the reverse situation may be the case whereby a mother's negative perception increases paternal anxiety.

Conversely, some studies have identified more positive factors for fathers associated with complicated childbirth. One study found that the mode of delivery (normal versus complicated) did not have an impact on the stress response of fathers (Skari et al, 2002). Another reported that fathers were reassured by the involvement of technology (Eriksson et al, 2006). Fathers attending an elective LSCS also felt more able to help their partner when compared to fathers attending normal and complicated emergency deliveries (Rosich-Medina and Shetty, 2007). No explanation of this finding is given. However, this may be because parents felt better prepared for the planned delivery. The mothers would also have been awake and pain-free during the birth and therefore more readily able to interact with their partner.

The father's needs

Although there is limited discussion in the literature about fathers' needs during complicated and preterm childbirth, three can be identified. Fathers have said that they need to understand what has happened and why (McCain and Deatrick, 1994; Alderson et al, 2006). They have also expressed the need to be present at the delivery because this confirms their identity as a father (Jackson et al, 2003; Lundqvist and Jakobsson, 2003). A final need that fathers have expressed is to share their feelings after the event with someone who has insight into their experiences (Koppel and Kaiser, 2001; Lindberg et al, 2007). However, it seems that these needs are often not met (Harvey, 2010). Fathers have reported that they experienced limited provision of information before, during or after complicated and preterm childbirth. They are sometimes unable to attend these types of birth because of institutional policies and procedures, and the opportunity for debriefing either with healthcare professionals, family or friends is also usually limited, and in many cases non-existent (Harvey, 2010).

A recent study included interviews with fathers and healthcare professionals and the observation of complicated births. It identified a specific situation that fathers may experience when complicated childbirth occurs, which highlights a father's need for information and support. This is when fathers had to wait, usually on their own, whilst preparations were made in the operating theatre for a complicated delivery (usually LSCS). As a consequence of hospital policy, fathers were unable to accompany their partner during this time and had to wait 20 to 60 minutes before being able to join their partner in the theatre.

Some fathers said this was the most distressing part of their entire experience, 'That was the hardest time, because I was just, I've never felt so alone really...probably the longest hour of my life' (Harvey, 2010: 124). Fathers felt the impact of the wait was made worse because they were alone, often without any information about what was happening. They felt abandoned during this time and often could not find anyone to ask what was happening. They did not want to move away from where they had been told to wait because they did not know when they would be called into the operating theatre. They also were unable to contact family and friends during this time to tell them what was happening because of restrictions regarding the use of mobile telephones in clinical areas. Conversely, other fathers had to wait in public areas where they felt they had to control their emotions whilst in the presence of others. They also did not want to make personal telephone calls in front of other people (Harvey, 2010).

Long-term impact

Events surrounding preterm and complicated childbirth are often recalled by fathers with clarity, regardless of the intervening period of time (Casimir, 1999; Jackson et al, 2003). There is, however, limited evidence regarding the long-term impact of these events on fathers. Traumatic childbirth (which may involve a complicated delivery) can have a negative impact on a father's future relationship with his partner or child (White, 2007). These harmful effects may be apparent years later and reported symptoms are synonymous with post-traumatic stress disorder (PTSD) (Chan and Paterson-Brown, 2002). Fathers have described experiencing flashbacks of complicated and preterm deliveries some time after the birth (Casimir, 1999; Harvey, 2012). The study undertaken by Parfitt and Ayers (2009) provides further insight: Both mothers and fathers had a generally negative perception of the birth with most reporting that it had been a worse experience than anticipated. However, this study specifically recruited parents who had experienced traumatic deliveries. Nevertheless, a higher incidence of PTSD was found in relation to emergency LSCS delivery in comparison to normal birth (Parfitt and Ayers, 2009). It would appear that there is scope for more extensive longitudinal research in this area.

Fathers encountering newborn resuscitation

The increasing incidence of preterm birth and the correlation between this type of delivery and newborn resuscitation (Confidential Enquiry into Stillbirths and Deaths in Infancy, 2003), means that more and more fathers are present during the resuscitation of their baby at delivery. Whilst 'resuscitation' can have a variety of definitions (Royal College of Nursing, 2002), in this context newborn resuscitation includes interventions such as intubation, bag and mask ventilation, the administration of face mask oxygen, chest compressions, oral and pharyngeal suctioning, the administration of drugs, and/or the use of infused fluids (volume expanders).

It is unclear exactly how many babies in the UK require this level of support at birth (Resuscitation Council, 2006). A decade ago it was stated that 0.5–1% of babies required intubation (Rennie and Roberton, 2002), but more recently it has been suggested that relatively few babies need any form of support at birth (Richmond and Wyllie, 2010). However, no current evidence is provided to substantiate either statement. A recent attempt to record the number of babies requiring intubation at delivery was abandoned because data were poorly documented (Healthcare Commission, 2008). This problem was also reported in a large national study where the decision was made not to collect data regarding newborn resuscitation because of concerns regarding data validity (Costeloe et al, 2000). Whatever the case, given the increased incidence of preterm birth, it is likely that, although the number of babies requiring resuscitation at birth in the UK is small, it is increasing. Babies are usually resuscitated in the delivery room, so most fathers who attend a birth will also be present during the resuscitation if this is required. This is in contrast to other care settings which, until the 1990s usually excluded relatives when a family member required resuscitation.

Over the past two decades 'witnessed resuscitation' has been introduced in many critical care settings such as accident and emergency departments and adult and paediatric intensive care. This strategy enables relatives to be present, if they wish, during the resuscitation of a family member. The introduction of this strategy often took place despite the initial reluctance of many healthcare professionals who felt that insufficient staff would be available to support relatives and that the equipment and lack of space would create unnecessary hazards (McGahey, 2002). It was also felt the presence of relatives would increase the risk of litigation and would have a negative effect on the healthcare professionals' ability to carry out the resuscitation safely and effectively (Schilling, 1994; Grice et al, 2003). It is interesting to note that similar arguments were used 50 years ago against the presence of fathers during childbirth. Nevertheless, witnessed resuscitation was gradually introduced and is now common practice in many critical care settings around the world. Over time, healthcare professionals have seen the benefits of this strategy and most have found ways to accommodate it in their practice. In much the same way, healthcare professionals have become accustomed to fathers attending childbirth to such an extent that it also has become common practice.

Witnessed resuscitation has been the focus of much research over the past two decades (van der Woning, 1999; Weslien et al, 2005). Whilst very little work specifically explores fathers' experiences of the resuscitation of their baby at birth (Harvey, 2012) the more general witnessed resuscitation literature raises both positive and negative issues that may apply when fathers attend the resuscitation of their baby. This literature has been combined and reviewed. Two key themes can be identified: 'impact on the relatives' and 'implications for service delivery'.

Impact on the relatives

Being present helps relatives understand what happened, reassures them that everything possible was done, and enables them to advocate for their family member (Grice et al, 2003; Maxton, 2008; Lippert et al, 2010). Being present also provides an opportunity to see, touch and speak to the family member. This is often important to relatives if the resuscitation is unsuccessful, and can help the subsequent grieving process (Royal College of Nursing, 2002; Grice et al, 2003; Baskett et al, 2005). For some relatives, being present during the resuscitation can be a distressing and overwhelming experience (Grice et al, 2003; Weslien et al, 2005). However, Maxton (2008) identified, in qualitative interviews with 14 parents, that they were not distressed by the resuscitation *per se* but rather by the fact that their child needed this level of support. As a consequence, some parents did not watch what was happening (Maxton, 2008). This response is reported elsewhere in an anecdotal account by a father who could not watch when his son was intubated and had to leave the room whilst an intravenous line was sited. This response is particularly striking because he was a doctor working in a paediatric intensive care unit at the time (Jenni, 2000). The dilemma over whether or not to watch the resuscitation is further endorsed by Lee et al's (2009) study of fathers' experiences of preterm birth. One father identified that although he did not want to watch the resuscitation, he did so because he thought he might not see his baby alive again.

Other negative issues occur for relatives when healthcare professionals over-use medical jargon and terminology and underplay what is happening during the resuscitation so that the relatives' understanding is compromised (Weslien et al, 2005; Maxton, 2008). This may be a deliberate and perhaps paternalistic strategy by healthcare professionals to reduce the relatives' anxiety. It may also be done with the intention of excluding the relatives. Alternatively, it may reveal the healthcare professionals' lack of confidence about breaking bad news or their uncertainty regarding their roles and responsibilities. However, it must be emphasised that although relatives feel frustrated by a lack of information at the time, they would rather the healthcare professionals focused their attention on the resuscitation (Maxton, 2008; Harvey, 2010, 2012).

Most relatives want to be with their family member during the resuscitation and those who were, felt in retrospect they were right to do this (Meyers et al, 1998; Robinson et al, 1998; Maxton, 2008). However, they worry about being in the way and also value being able to leave and return to the room during the resuscitation (Goldstein et al, 1997; Meyers et al, 1998; Maxton, 2008). This raises a question about what fathers would choose if given the opportunity. Most fathers who attend a birth will be present during the resuscitation because babies are usually resuscitated in the same room. They therefore have little choice about being present, unless they advocate for themselves or are asked if they would like to leave. Although Jenni (2000) describes leaving the room and returning, it is not known if fathers generally do this. In a study involving qualitative interviews with 20 fathers and 37 healthcare professionals, two accounts were given of fathers leaving the room during the baby's resuscitation (Harvey, 2010).

The long-term impact of witnessed resuscitation on relatives has not been explored extensively although the possibility that they may experience PTSD has been raised (van der Woning, 1999). A small-scale study that followed up relatives six months after the resuscitation found no evidence of psychological distress (Robinson et al, 1998). A more recent study of fathers' experiences indicated that a small number had nightmares and flashbacks about their baby's resuscitation (Harvey, 2012). It would appear that there is scope for more extensive longitudinal research in this area.

Implications for service delivery

Witnessed resuscitation has become accepted practice in critical care settings in many Western countries and has become the focus of various protocols, guidelines and recommendations to promote good practice (Royal College of Nursing, 2002; Lynch et al, 2008; Biarent et al, 2010). These identify that relatives should be briefed before going into the resuscitation area, chaperoned during the resuscitation, and should receive follow-up support afterwards (McGahey, 2002; Weslien et al, 2005; Lynch et al, 2008; Biarent et al, 2010). They should not, however, be pressurised to attend (Royal College of Nursing, 2002; Baskett et al, 2005). It is therefore important to determine relatives' views about attending in advance if at all possible (Grice et al, 2003; Lippert et al, 2010). The chaperone role should be undertaken by a senior healthcare professional, usually a nurse (Goldstein et al, 1997; Maxton, 2008).

These protocols, guidelines and recommendations could all be applied to situations when fathers attend newborn resuscitation. However, it is not known the extent to which any of these are addressed in practice. Whilst specific consideration has recently been given to neonatal resuscitation, it is unclear whether the recommendations apply to the delivery room (Lynch et al, 2008). More detailed guidance about newborn resuscitation in the delivery room is given in newborn life support courses for healthcare professionals. This guidance mainly focuses on communicating with the parents (Nolan et al, 2010; Resuscitation Council, 2011). It is also identified that parental needs should be respected and that parents should be encouraged to see, touch or hold their baby after the resuscitation, if this is appropriate (Nolan et al, 2010). However, no reference is made to ways in which the father can be specifically supported.

A study involving interviews with 20 fathers and 37 healthcare professionals, and the observation of deliveries involving newborn resuscitation, indicated that few of the more general protocols, guidelines and recommendations regarding witnessed resuscitation appeared to have been implemented. Most fathers could not recall being briefed about the resuscitation before the event. A few fathers remembered being given vague information, for example, that the baby may require 'help' to breathe at birth. They were not told, however, the possible nature and extent of this 'help'. Similarly, none of the fathers was debriefed about the resuscitation after the event (Harvey, 2010, 2012). Interviews with the healthcare professionals provided further insight. These revealed that none of the professional groups who were routinely present during newborn resuscitation (midwives, obstetricians, anaesthetists, paediatricians, neonatal nurses and neonatal nurse practitioners) felt it was part of their role to support fathers in this way. The fathers were also not chaperoned during the resuscitation. Interviews with healthcare professionals identified that whilst some were aware that this arrangement occurred in other critical care settings, none felt it was possible in this context, primarily because of a lack of resources (Harvey, 2010).

The dearth of literature regarding fathers' experiences of newborn resuscitation may be indicative of ethical and logistical problems surrounding research of this nature. It may also be the case that the experiences and perceptions of fathers have been regarded as being less important and not a priority in the organisation and delivery of care. It has taken two decades for witnessed resuscitation to become accepted practice in other critical care settings. Within the context of childbirth, fathers have been attending newborn resuscitation ever since they have routinely attended childbirth. The potential impact of this on fathers appears not to have previously been questioned.

Strategies to engage and involve fathers when adverse events occur during childbirth

The increasing incidence of complicated and preterm birth and newborn resuscitation brings an additional dimension to the drive to engage and involve fathers during childbirth. The involvement of a father in his child's life has long-term social and economic benefit not only for the father himself but also for the child, the mother, and society in general (Beardshaw, 2001; Friedewald et al, 2005). Pregnancy and childbirth provide ideal opportunities to promote this involvement (Burgess, 2008). It is therefore imperative that any detrimental effects that a father may experience as a consequence of being present during childbirth are minimised. In so doing, the likelihood of long-term problems associated with absent fathers, or psychological problems such as PTSD that may jeopardise a father's future relationship with his partner and/or child, should be reduced (Sullivan-Lyons, 1998; Mander, 2004; Parfitt and Ayers, 2009). It is therefore important that healthcare professionals and the wider service look for ways to minimise these detrimental effects. This can be done by ensuring the provision of maternity and neonatal care that includes and supports the needs of fathers, in addition to those of mothers and babies.

Most fathers want to play a constructive role around the time of the birth of their baby. Their ability and opportunity to do this can be enhanced through guidance, support and encouragement from healthcare professionals. This group may include midwives, obstetricians, anaesthetists, paediatricians, neonatal nurse practitioners and neonatal nurses. Whilst individual practitioners representing these professional groups may feel the following strategies are already encompassed within their practice, evidence suggests that for many fathers this is not always the case (Harvey, 2010). The service influences to some extent the ways in which healthcare professionals work, but consideration of these strategies provides an opportunity for individuals to reflect on ways in which their own practice could be enhanced. These strategies could be employed during the antenatal period, at delivery or immediately afterwards. Whilst some strategies relate specifically to the provision of information, others focus on more general aspects of care. Although many of these strategies would equally apply in relation to normal childbirth, they are presented here in the context of complicated and preterm birth and situations where newborn resuscitation is required.

Healthcare professionals could emphasise the importance of antenatal preparation for fatherhood when problems are identified during the pregnancy which indicate that complicated or preterm childbirth and/or newborn resuscitation are likely to occur. Recommendations could be made regarding books to read and/or websites to access. Advising prospective fathers that it is quite common for them to feel powerless at some point, even during normal childbirth (Draper, 2003; Rosich-Medina and Shetty, 2007) may help them cope more effectively with these feelings during and immediately after the birth. Healthcare professionals could also discuss with fathers the possibility that they will feel conflict about who they should feel most worried about: their partner or their baby, when adverse events occur (Koppel and Kaiser, 2001; Lindberg et al, 2007). This may help to reduce any subsequent feelings of guilt and remorse.

Healthcare professionals could encourage fathers to think in advance about their own support needs and in particular the value of having a family member or friend as a 'point of contact' (Schwarzer et al, 2004). The importance of family, friends and work colleagues 'behind the scenes' should not be underestimated (Sarafino, 2006; Deave et al, 2008). These people can play an important, but often unseen role supporting both the psychological and physical needs of fathers. One of the surprising findings of a recent study of fathers' experiences of adverse events occurring around the time of the birth of their baby was the key role the father's own father played (Harvey, 2010). Absence of the extended family and the increasing numbers of fractured and reconfigured families may increasingly limit opportunities for support provided by family members, thus making a father's support from friends and work colleagues all the more important.

If time permits before the delivery and/or resuscitation, discussion with the father should illicit the extent to which he would like to be included during and immediately after the birth. This should reveal his preferred style of coping. Some fathers may want to be involved and fully informed whilst others would rather take a 'back seat' and prefer not to be told what is happening. In many situations the most straightforward way to ensure a father's needs are met is to ask him his preferences at the outset. However, this should be done in a way that ensures that he feels he genuinely has a choice. During the subsequent birth and resuscitation the father's preferred style of coping should be respected and his level of involvement not viewed in a negative way. In cases where a father wants to be actively involved, opportunities should be taken to guide him on the appropriate ways in which he might do this.

During the resuscitation, all fathers should be enabled to take 'time-out' and leave the room if they wish (Goldstein et al, 1997; Jenni, 2000; Maxton, 2008). This may involve helping the father to negotiate his way past equipment and other people who may be present at the time. Healthcare professionals could volunteer or nominate another colleague to support the father during the resuscitation, as is the case in other care settings (Goldstein et al, 1997; Baskett et al, 2005). This may include taking him to the resuscitaire and encouraging him to touch his baby (Jackson et al, 2003). Healthcare professionals could also offer the opportunity to discuss what happened after the event in the form of a formal or informal debriefing. Once the resuscitation has been completed, healthcare professionals could take the opportunity to advocate for the father, ensuring he has an opportunity to touch or hold his baby if this is what he wishes (Bliss, 2009).

Several strategies for healthcare professionals to consider relate to the process of information giving. These include explaining beforehand about what might happen at the birth (Ryan, 2009), maintaining eye contact, and the judicious use of non-verbal communication. Fathers often observe the non-verbal communication between healthcare professionals in order to ascertain what is happening (Harvey, 2012). Healthcare professionals should also reflect on the possible effect of what they do not say. For example, fathers often assume that they cannot go to their baby on the resuscitaire because they are not invited to do so (Harvey, 2010). Paediatricians and neonatal nurse practitioners should also speak to both parents about their baby's care before they leave the delivery room, irrespective of the baby's need for resuscitation (Nolan et al, 2010; Resuscitation Council, 2011). Some healthcare professionals have expressed uncertainty about the nature, extent and timing of information that they should give to fathers before, during and after adverse events (Harvey, 2010). It appears that decisions about this important aspect of care are usually left to individual practitioners. Whilst it would not be appropriate to be too prescriptive, there is scope for the development of broad guidelines that could facilitate this process.

More general strategies include recognising the value that fathers place on receiving information about their partner and baby from the senior healthcare professionals who were involved in their care (Harvey, 2010). Juniors may therefore need to advocate on behalf of fathers to ensure that they have opportunities to discuss issues with their more senior colleagues. Individual healthcare professionals could also reflect on their personal philosophy of care, in particular the extent to which they demonstrate a family-centred approach and whether they feel they have a duty of care to the father (Department of Health, 2009; Ryan, 2009). When adverse events occur, the father's experience is often shaped by what he is not 'allowed' to do (Draper, 1997), such as not being able to be with his partner whilst preparations are made in the operating theatre for LSCS or being unable to go to his baby on the resuscitaire. Healthcare professionals can help fathers to gain a level of control over their experience by suggesting ways in which they can support their partner, by keeping them fully informed and by involving them in decision-making processes.

There are also strategies that those responsible for the wider service could put in place to ensure the needs of fathers are more adequately met. In this context, this includes those with managerial responsibility in local trusts and networks and policy makers at both local and national levels. There should be a focus on the ways in which care and support for fathers may be enhanced and this should include strategies that could be employed before the birth, the provision of resources for fathers within the care setting, staffing levels, healthcare staff training and professional development, and philosophies of care.

The accessibility, timing and content regarding fatherhood in parentcraft classes should be reviewed at both a local and national level. Concern has been expressed about the reduced availability of this resource over recent years (Clift-Matthews, 2007; Bainbridge, 2009). This is contrary to the ethos of recent directives to engage and involve fathers during pregnancy (Department of Health and Department for Education and Skills, 2004; Department of Health, 2009). Greater availability and flexibility of delivery would enable more fathers to attend classes. Many of these programmes take place in the daytime when fathers are unable to participate (Deave et al, 2008; Mottram, 2008). The inclusion of content regarding preterm birth, complicated childbirth and newborn resuscitation may be worthwhile. Running specific classes for parents when these types of event are predicted may be resource-intensive and logistically difficult to organise. It may also be difficult to meet the needs of individual parents unless provided by contact on a one-to-one basis. However, these factors should not preclude prospective parents having access to classes that meet their needs in a more effective way. The utilisation of alternative means by which to provide information such as online resources and DVDs should be considered (Dartnell et al, 2005; Bliss, 2009).

Several strategies relate to the availability of resources for fathers. The importance of somewhere private for fathers to take 'time-out', overnight accommodation and facilities for fathers to shower and change have been identified (Bliss, 2009; Department of Health, 2009). The provision of overnight accommodation for families is common in child health services and has been established for fathers in some maternity care settings (Bennett, 2011). There is, however, scope for this to be much more extensive. There is also scope to consider the provision of information regarding resources and sources of support for fathers within NHS trusts. Similar types of resources could also be made available for relatives about ways in which they can support fathers when these sorts of situations occur. There could be a benefit in producing these and other information in a variety of formats, such as audio or web-based material in addition to the more traditional written format (Dartnell et al, 2005; Bliss 2009).

To ensure a truly family-centred approach to care, the calculation of staffing levels and skill mix should take into consideration the needs of fathers, in addition to the needs of mothers and babies. Lack of available personnel to implement the chaperone role was initially cited when witnessed resuscitation was proposed in other critical care settings. However, this has now become common practice. The recruitment of additional personnel such as someone to chaperone fathers during the resuscitation of their baby at delivery should also therefore be considered (Grice et al, 2003; Baskett et al, 2005). Ways in which the engagement and involvement of fathers could be enhanced within the overall philosophy of care within the care setting could also be considered. A family-centred philosophy of care that is evident throughout the service should provide seamless, integrated care and support for fathers. Care settings therefore need to go beyond the endorsement of the philosophy, and ensure it is implemented. It is likely this will require additional resources, staff training and a review of policies and procedures (Peterson et al, 2004; Ryan, 2009). Finally, meeting fathers' needs should also feature more prominently in midwifery, obstetric, paediatric and neonatal training, and professional development programmes, particularly in relation to information-giving during adverse events and supporting fathers more effectively.

Conclusion

Childbirth is a major life event for most fathers. Whilst for many men these events are straightforward, for some this is not the case. Preterm and complicated childbirth and newborn resuscitation are events in which fathers are increasingly involved (Murphy et al, 2004; Langhoff-Roos et al, 2006; Healthcare Commission, 2008). Despite changing trends in the presence and involvement of fathers in childbirth over the past 50 years, an increasing awareness of the need to engage and involve fathers in all aspects of their child's life (Beardshaw, 2001; Burgess, 2008) and recent initiatives to involve fathers during childbirth (Department of Health and Department for Education and Skills, 2004; National Institute for Health and Clinical Excellence, 2006), the impact of childbirth on fathers has not been extensively considered. This is particularly the case when adverse events occur. A decade ago, it was asserted that fathers often did not have a place in the maternity care system (Early, 2001). Ten years on, the situation appears in many respects to be largely unchanged. Failing to meet the needs of fathers is even more likely, when adverse events occur around the time of the baby's birth (Harvey, 2010, 2012).

Key points

- Most fathers in the UK attend the birth and immediate care of their baby. This includes normal, complicated and preterm deliveries and situations when the baby requires resuscitation at birth
- Most research exploring men's experiences of childbirth has focused on the fathers of healthy babies who were born at term by normal delivery
- Fathers who attend the birth of their baby experience a range of positive and negative emotions. They are unclear of their role and experience limited support from healthcare professionals before, during or after the birth
- The needs of fathers are often not adequately considered in the configuration and provision of maternity and neonatal services
- Fathers who are present during the resuscitation of their baby at birth do not appear to be afforded the level of care and support available to relatives who witness the resuscitation of a family member in other critical care settings
- There is a need for more extensive, longitudinal studies to determine the long-term impact on fathers of being present during adverse childbirth events

---

Case history I
Normal, preterm delivery

Jo is in labour at 35 weeks' gestation. This is her second child; her daughter is 8 years old. Jo's partner is Ben and this is his first child. Jo coped well with her early labour and spent most of the time between her contractions chatting with Sarah, the midwife. Jo's contractions have now become stronger and more frequent. She is using entonox and rests quietly on the bed between contractions.

Ben has been with Jo throughout her six hour labour but appears uninterested in what is happening. He frequently leaves the room. At other times he sits in the far corner of the room sending text messages and reading the newspaper. Sarah, the midwife is becoming increasingly frustrated by Ben's behaviour.

Jo now appears to be approaching the second stage of her labour. Sarah tells Jo and Ben that a paediatrician must attend the delivery and that the baby may require admission to the neonatal unit. They had not previously been told about this and Jo becomes distressed. Ben becomes more engaged with what is happening. He is agitated and starts asking a lot of questions. Jo's labour is now advancing rapidly, she is pushing and the vertex is visible. Sarah focuses her attention on Jo and most of Ben's questions go unanswered. Ben tries to comfort his partner but Sarah tells Jo to concentrate on her and to follow her instructions. Sarah calls for assistance and another midwife and the paediatrician arrive. Ben moves to the corner of the room. A baby girl is delivered by normal delivery. The baby cries lustily and Jo holds her. Sarah notices that Ben is crying, but does not speak to him.

Reflective questions

- What might Ben have been thinking and feeling during the early part of Jo's labour?
- What strategies could Sarah have used to engage and involve Ben during Jo's labour?
- What might Ben have been thinking and feeling immediately before the delivery and once his daughter was born?
- How could Sarah have prepared Ben and Jo for the delivery and immediate care of their baby?
- To what extent does this scenario reflect the experiences of fathers in your practice area? Are the experiences of fathers encountering this sort of situation controlled or facilitated?
- What additional strategies could be implemented to improve the experiences of fathers who encounter this sort of scenario in your practice area?

Case history 2
Emergency LSCS and newborn resuscitation

Alan and his partner Samina are expecting their first baby. Samina went into labour at 40 weeks and 6 days gestation following spontaneous rupture of membranes. The decision to deliver the baby by emergency caesarean section is made following concern regarding fetal wellbeing monitoring (CTG trace) during labour. Samina and Alan are told that an emergency LSCS is required. The possibility that the baby might need resuscitation is not mentioned. Samina already has an epidural *in situ* and is taken to the operating theatre. Alan is told that he will be able to attend the delivery but must wait in the recovery area whilst preparations are made in theatre. During the time that he waits on his own, no-one from the healthcare team speaks to him. Twenty minutes later, Lizzie, the midwife who is caring for Samina, takes Alan to theatre and tells him to sit on the stool that is positioned close to Samina. Only the anaesthetist acknowledges that Alan has come into the theatre. As Alan holds Samina's hand, he listens to the conversations between the healthcare team. He hears someone say, 'We need to get this baby out now.' As the baby is delivered someone else says. 'It's a boy.' Alan stands up to see what is happening. The anaesthetist tells him to sit down. The baby does not cry. Alan asks what is happening, but no-one answers. Samina starts to cry. The baby is taken to the resuscitaire in the far corner of the room and Alan stands up again. He is told once more, to sit down. During the next 10 minutes various people come in and out of the operating theatre, none of them speak to Samina or Alan. Alan tries to listen to the muffled conversations between the healthcare team, but he cannot hear what they are saying. The anaesthetist starts to chat to Samina and Alan and tells them that their baby 'needs a bit of help to breathe'. After a while, the baby starts to cry. Lizzie brings the baby over and gives him to Alan to hold. Lizzie does not give them any information about what has happened. Instead, she says that the doctor will speak to them about the baby, but the paediatrician leaves the operating theatre without doing so.

Reflective questions

* What might Alan have been thinking and feeling whilst he waited in the recovery area?
* What might Alan have been thinking and feeling during the delivery and resuscitation of his baby?

- How could the healthcare team have prepared Alan for the delivery and immediate care of his baby? Which members of the healthcare team should provide this support?
- What could the healthcare team have done to support Alan during the preparation for the delivery, the delivery itself and the resuscitation of his baby? Which members of the healthcare team should provide this support?
- To what extent does this scenario reflect the experiences of fathers in your practice area? Are the experiences of fathers encountering this sort of situation controlled or facilitated?
- What additional strategies could be implemented to improve the experiences of fathers who encounter this sort of scenario in your practice area?

References

Alderson P, Hawthorne J, Killen M (2006) Parents' experiences of sharing neonatal information and decisions: Consent, cost and risk. *Social Science and Medicine* **62**: 1319–29

Bainbridge J (2009) Equal access to high-quality antenatal classes. *British Journal of Midwifery* **17**: 457–8

Baskett PJF, Steen PA, Bossaert L (2005) European Resuscitation Council Guidelines for Resuscitation 2005 - Section 8. The ethics of resuscitation and end-of-life decisions. *Resuscitation* **67**: S171–80

Beardshaw T (2001) Supporting the role of fathers around the time of birth. *MIDIRS Midwifery Digest* **11**: 476–9

Bedford VA, Johnson N (1988) The role of the father. *Midwifery* **4**: 190–5

Bennett R (2011) Won't you stay the night? *Midwives* **2**: 32–4

Berry LM (1988) Realistic expectations of the labor coach. *Journal of Obstetric, Gynecologic and Neonatal Nursing* **Sept/Oct** : 354–5

Biarent D, Bingham R, Eich C, et al (2010) European Resuscitation Council Guidelines for Resuscitation 2010: Section 6. Paediatric life support. *Resuscitation* **81**: 1364–88

Bliss (2009) *The Bliss Baby Charter Standards*. Bliss, London

Bondas-Salonen T (1998) How women experience the presence of their partners at the births of their babies. *Qualitative Health Research* **8**: 784–800

Brown A (1982) Fathers in the labour ward: Medical and lay accounts. In: McKee L, O'Brien M (eds) *The father figure*. Tavistock Publications, London

Burgess A (1997) *Fatherhood reclaimed: The making of the modern father*. Vermillion, London

Burgess A (2008) *Maternal and infant health in the perinatal period: The father's role.* The Fatherhood Institute, Abergavenny

Calam RM, Lambrenos K, Cox AD, Weindling AM (1999) Maternal appraisal of information given around the time preterm delivery. *Journal of Reproductive and Infant Psychology* **17**: 267–80

Casimir J (1999) *Naomi's story.* Allen and Unwin, St Leonards

Castle H, Slade P, Barranco-Wadlow M, Rogers M (2008) Attitudes to emotional expression, social support and postnatal adjustment in new parents. *Journal of Reproductive and Infant Psychology* **26**: 195–210

Chalmers B, Meyer D (1996) What men say about pregnancy, birth and parenthood. *Journal of Psychosomatic Obstetrics and Gynecology* **17**: 47–52

Chan KKL, Paterson-Brown S (2002) How do fathers feel after accompanying their partners in labour and delivery? *Journal of Obstetrics and Gynaecology* **22**: 11–15

Chandler S, Field PA (1997) Becoming a father: First-time fathers' experience of labor and delivery. *Journal of Nurse-Midwifery* **42**: 17–24

Chapman LL (1992) Expectant fathers' roles during labor and birth. *Journal of Obstetric, Gynecologic and Neonatal Nursing* **21**: 114–20

Clift-Matthews V (2007) Maternity services suffer again. *British Journal of Midwifery* **15**: 184

Condon JT, Boyce P, Corkindale CJ (2004) The first-time fathers study: A prospective study of the mental health and well-being of men during the transition to parenthood. *Australian and New Zealand Journal of Psychiatry* **38**: 56–64

Confidential Enquiry into Stillbirths and Deaths in Infancy (2003) *Project 27/28: An enquiry into quality of care and its effect on the survival of babies born at 27–28 weeks.* The Stationery Office, Norwich

Costeloe K, Hennessy E, Gibson AT, Marlow N, Wilkinson AR (2000) The EPICure Study: Outcomes to discharge from hospital for infants born at the threshold of viability. *Pediatrics* **106**: 659–71

Cronenwett LR, Newmark LL (1974) Fathers' responses to childbirth. *Nursing Research* **23**: 210–17

Dartnell L, Ganguly N, Batterham J (2005) *Access to maternity services research report.* Department of Health, London

Deave T, Johnson D, Ingram J (2008) The transition to parenthood: The needs of parents in pregnancy and early parenthood. *BMC Pregnancy and Childbirth* **8**(30): 1–11

Department of Health (2009) *Toolkit for high-quality neonatal services.* Department of Health, London

Department of Health, Department for Education and Skills (2004) *National service framework for children, young people and maternity services: Maternity.* Department of Health, London

Donnison J (1988) *Midwives and medical men: A history of the struggle for the control of childbirth* (2nd edn). Historical Publications, London

Draper J (1997) Whose welfare in the labour room? A discussion of the increasing trend of fathers' birth attendance. *Midwifery* **13**: 132–8

Draper J (2003) Men's passage to fatherhood: An analysis of the contemporary relevance of transition theory. *Nursing Inquiry* **10**: 66–78

Early R (2001) Men as consumers of maternity services: A contradiction in terms. *International Journal of Consumer Studies* **25**: 160–7

Enkin M, Keirse MJNC, Neilson J et al (2000) A guide to effective care in pregnancy (3rd edn). Oxford University Press, Oxford

Eriksson C, Westman G, Hamberg K (2006) Content of childbirth-related fear in Swedish women and men – analysis of an open-ended question. *Journal of Midwifery and Women's Health* **51**: 112–18

Fägerskiöld A (2008) A change in life as experienced by first-time fathers. *Scandinavian Journal of Caring Science* **22**: 64–71

Foyster EA (1999) *Manhood in early modern England: Honour, sex and marriage.* Longman, London

Francis M (2002) The domestication of the male? Recent research on nineteenth and twentieth-century British masculinity. *Historical Journal* **45**(3): 637–52

Friedewald M, Fletcher R, Fairbairn H (2005) All-male discussion forums for expectant fathers: Evaluation of a model. *Journal of Perinatal Education* **14**(2): 8–18

Goebel N (2004) High dependency midwifery care – does it make a difference? *MIDIRS Midwifery Digest* **14**: 221–6

Goldstein A, Berry K, Callaghan A (1997) Resuscitation witnessed by relatives has proved acceptable to doctors in paediatric cases. *British Medical Journal* **314**: 144–5

Greenhalgh R, Slade P, Spiby H (2000) Fathers' coping style, antenatal preparation and experiences of labor and the postpartum. *Birth* **27**: 177–84

Grice AS, Picton P, Deakin CDS (2003) Study examining attitudes of staff, paediatrics and relatives to witnessed resuscitation in adult intensive care units. *British Journal of Anaesthesia* **91**: 820–4

Gungor I, Beji NK (2007) Effects of fathers' attendance to labor and delivery on the experience of childbirth in Turkey. *Western Journal of Nursing Research* **29**: 213–31

Harvey ME (2010) *The experiences and perceptions of fathers attending the birth and immediate care of their baby.* Unpublished PhD Thesis: Aston University, Birmingham

Harvey ME (2012) Being there: A qualitative interview study with fathers present during the resuscitation of their baby at delivery. *Archives of Disease in Childhood – Fetal and Neonatal Edition* doi:10.1136/archdischild-2011-301482

Healthcare Commission (2008) *Towards better births.* Commission for Healthcare Audit and Inspection, London

Hildingsson I, Häggström T (1999) Midwives' lived experiences of being supportive to prospective mothers/parents during pregnancy. *Midwifery* **15**: 82–91

Hodnett ED, Gates S, Hofmeyer GJ, Sakala C, Weston J (2011) Continuous support for women during childbirth. *Cochrane Database Systematic Reviews* Issue 2 Art No.: CD003766. DOI:10.1002/14651858.CD003766.pub3

Jackson B (1983) *Fatherhood*. George Allen & Unwin, London

Jackson K, Ternestedt B-M, Schollin J (2003) From alienation to familiarity: Experiences of mothers and fathers of preterm babies. *Journal of Advanced Nursing* **43**: 120–9

Jacoby A (1987) Women's preferences for and satisfaction with current procedures in childbirth – Findings from a national study. *Midwifery* **3**: 117–24

Jenni OG (2000) On the other side of the tracks. *The Lancet* **355**: 139–40

Johnson MP (2002) The implications of unfulfilled expectations and perceived pressure to attend the birth on men's stress levels following birth attendance: A longitudinal study. *Journal of Psychosomatic Obstetrics and Gynecology* **23**: 173–82

Keogh E, Hughes S, Ellery D, Daniel C, Holdcroft A. (2005) Psychological influences on women's experience of planned elective cesarean section. *Psychosomatic Medicine* **68**: 167–74

Kiernan K, Smith K (2003) *Unmarried parenthood: New insights from the Millennium Cohort Study*. In: Office for National Statistics Population Trends. Winter 2003 114. The Stationary Office, London

Klaus MH, Kennell JH (1982) *Parent–infant bonding* (2nd edn). CV Mosby, St. Louis MO

Klein RP, Gist NF, Nicholson J, Standley K (1981) A study of father and nurse support during labor. *Birth and the Family Journal* **8**: 161–4

Koppel GT, Kaiser D (2001) Fathers at the end of their rope: A brief report on fathers abandoned in the perinatal situation. *Journal of Reproductive and Infant Psychology* **19**: 249–51

Kunjappy-Clifton A (2008) And father came too.... a study exploring the role of first time fathers during the birth process and to explore the meaning of the experience for these men: Part two. *MIDIRS Midwifery Digest* **18**: 57–66

Langhoff-Roos J, Kesmodel U, Jacobsson B, Rasmussen S, Vogel I (2006) Spontaneous preterm delivery in primiparous women at low risk in Denmark: Population based study. *British Medical Journal* **332**: 937–9

Lee T-Y, Lin H-R, Huang T-H, Hsu C-H, Bartlett R (2009) Assuring the integrity of the family: Being the family of a very low birth weight infant. *Journal of Clinical Nursing* **18**: 512–19

Leavitt JW (2003) What do men have to do with it? Fathers and mid-twentieth century childbirth. *Bulletin of the History of Medicine* **77**(2): 235-62

Lindberg B, Axelsson K, Öhrling K (2007) The birth of premature infants: Experiences from the fathers' perspective. *Journal of Neonatal Nursing* **13**: 142–9

Lippert FK, Raffay, V, Georgiou M, Steen PA, Bossaert L (2010) European Resuscitation Council Guidelines for Resuscitation 2010 - Section 10. The ethics of resuscitation and end-of-life decisions. *Resuscitation* **81**: 1445–51

Longworth H (2006) Should fathers be in the labour room? Yes, for support not intervention. *British Journal of Midwifery* **1**(4): 288

Longworth HL, Kingdon CK (2011) fathers in the birth room: What are they expecting and experiencing? A phenomenological study. *Midwifery* **27**: 588-94

Lundqvist P, Jakobsson L (2003) Swedish men's experiences of becoming fathers to their preterm infants. *Neonatal Network* **22**(6): 25–31

Lynch F, Fulbrook P, Latour J, et al (2008) The presence of family members during cardiopulmonary resuscitation: Position statement. *Infant* **4**(2): 44–5

McCain GC, Deatrick JA (1994) The experience of high-risk pregnancy. *Journal of Obstetric, Gynecologic and Neonatal Nursing* **23**: 421–7

McGahey PR (2002) Family presence during pediatric resuscitation: Focus on staff. *Critical Care Nurse* **22**(6): 29–34

Mander R (2004) *Men and maternity.* Routledge, London

Maternal Critical Care Working Group (2011) *Providing equity of critical and maternity care for the critically ill pregnant or recently pregnant woman.* Royal College of Anaesthetists, London

Maxton FJC (2008) Parental presence during resuscitation in the PICU: The parents' experience. *Journal of Clinical Nursing* **17**: 3168–76

Meyers TA, Eichorn DJ, Guzzetta CE (1998) Do families want to be present during CPR? A retrospective survey. *Journal of Emergency Nursing* **24**: 400–5

Montigny de F, Lacharité C (2004) Fathers' perceptions of the immediate postpartal period. *Journal of Obstetric, Gynecologic and Neonatal Nursing* **33**: 328–38

Morse CA, Buist A, Durkin S (2000) First-time parenthood: Influences on pre- and postnatal adjustment in fathers and mothers. *Journal of Psychosomatic Obstetrics and Gynecology* 21: 109–20

Mottram L (2008) First-time expectant fathers and their influence on decision making regarding choice for place of birth. *MIDIRS Midwifery Digest* **18**: 582–9

Murphy DJ, Fowlie PW, McGuire W (2004) Obstetric issues in preterm birth. *British Medical Journal* **329**: 783–6

Murphy DJ, Pope C, Frost J, Liebling RE, (2003) Women's views on the impact of operative delivery in the second stage of labour: Qualitative interview study. *British Medical Journal* **327**: 1132–5

National Institute for Health and Clinical Excellence (2006) *Routine postnatal care of women and their babies.* National Institute for Health and Clinical Excellence, London

Nolan M (1996) One labour: Two very different experiences. *Modern Midwife* **6**(2): 6–9

Nolan JP, Soar J, Zidemanc DA, et al (2010) European Resuscitation Council Guidelines for Resuscitation 2010 Section1 Executive summary. *Resuscitation* **81**: 1219-76

Oakley A, Richards M (1990) Women's experiences of caesarean delivery. In: Garcia

J, Kilpatrick R, Richards M (eds) *The politics of maternity care.* Clarendon Press, Oxford

Odent M (1999) Is the participation of the father at birth dangerous? *Midwifery Today* **51**: 23–4

Odent M (2008) Dispelling the disempowering birth vocabulary. *Primal Health Research* **15**(4): 1–8

O'Malley M (2009) Should fathers be present at childbirth? *Midwives* **Dec/Jan**: 15

Parfitt YM, Ayers S (2009) The effect of post-natal symptoms of post-traumatic stress and depression on the couple's relationship and parent–baby bond. *Journal of Reproductive and Infant Psychology* **27**: 127–42

Peterson SW (2008) Father surrogate: Historical perceptions and perspectives of men in nursing and their relationship with fathers in the NICU. *Neonatal Network* **27**: 239–43

Peterson MF, Cohen J, Parsons V (2004) Family-centred care: Do we practice what we preach? *Journal of Obstetric, Gynaecologic and Neonatal Nursing* **33**: 421–27

Premberg A, Carlsson G, Hellstrom A-L, Berg M (2011) First-timer fathers' experiences of childbirth – a phenomenological study. *Midwifery* **27**: 848-53

Redshaw ME, Rowe R, Hockley C, Brocklehurst P (2007) *Recorded delivery: A national survey of women's experience of maternity care 2006.* NPEU, Oxford

Rennie JM, Roberton NRC (2002) *A manual of neonatal intensive care* (4th edn). Arnold, London

Resuscitation Council (2006) *Resuscitation at birth* (2nd edn). Resuscitation Council, London

Resuscitation Council (2011) *Resuscitation at birth* (3rd edn). Resuscitation Council, London

Richmond S, Wyllie J (2010) European Resuscitation Council Guidelines for Resuscitation 2010 - Section 7. Resuscitation of babies at birth. *Resuscitation* **81**: 1389–99

Robinson SM, Mackenzie-Ross S, Campbell Hewson GL, Egleston CV, Prevost AT (1998) Psychological effect of witnessed resuscitation on bereaved relatives. *The Lancet* **352**: 614–17

Rosich-Medina A, Shetty A (2007) Paternal experiences of pregnancy and labour. *British Journal of Midwifery* **15**: 66–74

Royal College of Nursing (2002) *Witnessing resuscitation.* Royal College of Nursing, London

Ryan N (2009) Stepping outside the medical treatment. *Midwives* **Dec**: 46

Ryding EL, Wijma K, Wijma B (2000) Emergency caesarean section: 25 women's experiences. *Journal of Reproductive and Infant Psychology* **18**: 33–9

Sarafino EP (2006) *Health psychology: Biopsychosocial interactions* (5th edn). John Wiley and Sons, Hoboken

Schilling RJ (1994) Should relatives watch resuscitation? No room for spectators. *British Medical Journal* **309**: 406

Schwarzer R, Knoll N, Rieckmann N (2004) Social support. In: Kaptein A, Weinman J (eds) *Health psychology.* BPS Blackwell, Oxford

Shribman S (2007) *Making it better: For mother and baby.* Department of Health, London

Simkin P (1992) Just another day in a woman's life? Part II: Nature and consistency of women's long-term memories of their first birth experiences. *Birth* **19**: 64–81

Singh D, Newburn M (2003) What men think of midwives. *Midwives* **6**: 70–4

Skari H, Skreden M, Malt UF, et al (2002) Comparative levels of psychological distress, symptoms, depression and anxiety after childbirth – a prospective population-based study of mothers and fathers. *British Journal of Obstetrics and Gynaecology* **109**: 1154–63

Somers-Smith MJ (1999) A place for the partner? Expectations and experiences of support during childbirth. *Midwifery* **15**: 101–8

Sullivan-Lyons J (1998) Men becoming fathers: 'Sometimes I wonder how I'll cope.' In: Clement S (ed) *Psychological perspectives on pregnancy and childbirth.* Churchill Livingstone, Edinburgh

Taylor IR, Bullough AS, van Hamel JCM, Campbell DNC (2002) Partner anxiety prior to elective caesarean section under regional anaesthesia. *Anaesthesia* **57**: 600–5

TNS System Three (2005) *NHS maternity services quantitative research.* TNS System Three, Edinburgh

van der Woning M (1999) Relatives in the resuscitation area: A phenomenological study. *Nursing in Critical Care* **4**: 186–92

Vehviläinen-Julkunen K, Liukkonen A (1998) Fathers' experiences of childbirth. *Midwifery* **14**: 10–17

Weslien M, Nilstun T, Lundqvist A, Fridlund B (2005) When the unreal becomes real: Family members' experiences of cardiac arrest. *British Association of Critical Care Nurses, Nursing in Critical Care* **10**: 15–22

White G (2007) You cope by breaking down in private: Fathers and PTSD following childbirth. *British Journal of Midwifery* **15**: 39–45

Wöckel A, Schäfer E, Beggel A, Abou-Dakn M (2007) Getting ready for birth: Impending fatherhood. *British Journal of Midwifery* **15**: 344–8

World Health Organization (2007) *Fatherhood and health outcomes in Europe.* World Health Organization, Copenhagen

Chapter 5

Fathers in the early postnatal period

Kevin Hugill

Introduction

After the emotionally charged experience of birth, fatherhood moves from abstract imagery to concrete reality, and fathers' ideas about fatherhood become reshaped by these experiences. This chapter draws attention to fathers in the early postnatal period following term and preterm birth. Evidence regarding fathers' experiences and their emotional responses to term and preterm birth are explored, together with strategies that could be used to engage with and involve fathers more readily during this period. The chapter ends with two case histories that aim to facilitate reflection on fathers' experiences and the ways in which fathers can be supported.

Fatherhood has changed in significant and measurable ways in the past 50 years. In part these changes reflect the changing status of women in society but also they reflect men's aspiration for greater involvement in the lives of their children. For many men, fatherhood is undoubtedly a considerable source of self-esteem and fulfilment (Erlandsson and Lindgren, 2009). There is an emerging consensus that fatherhood experiences have a profound effect upon men's identities and their perceptions of family roles (Burgess, 1997; Eggebean and Knoester, 2001; Deave and Johnson, 2008; Fägerskiöld, 2008). The time shortly after birth is a period of transition during which fathers seek to establish relationships and attachments to their newly born children. According to a number of sources (Henwood and Procter, 2003; Hamilton and deJonge, 2010) fathers can face unique and unsettling challenges during this time as they begin to navigate their way towards successful fatherhood. Unfortunately, men's preparation for fatherhood, how they manage the sometimes contradictory demands of fatherhood and their own needs in the early postnatal period, have only been partially studied and considerable gaps in our understanding remain.

Previous chapters have highlighted the intense emotional nature of many fathers' descriptions of events surrounding pregnancy and childbirth and how unprepared they feel for the experiences that childbirth affords them. This emotionality and lack of preparedness is widespread in fathers' accounts and continues into the postnatal period and beyond, both in general (Henderson and Brouse, 1991; McVeigh et al, 2002; White, 2007; Erlandsson et al, 2008;

Premberg et al, 2008) and in neonatal units (Lundqvist and Jakobsson, 2003; Arockiasamy et al, 2007; Lindberg et al 2007; Hugill, 2009). Emotions and how they are managed form an important aspect of the experience of fatherhood. Healthcare practitioners can help fathers by appreciating their unique emotions and how they try to control them during this time.

In *Chapter 4* it was stressed that most fathers now attend the birth of their children and that their roles and contributions during this time have continued to change. Similarly, fathers' roles, behaviours and expectations in the postnatal period have also changed over similar timescales. This somewhat fluid and dynamic situation continues to affect men's participation and contributions to family life. Fatherhood is a life-long experience but most research concerning fathers' relationships with their children has focused on early stages of the life cycle; the period from birth to adolescence. Fathers' relationships with their older adult children have been largely ignored; nevertheless the nature of these ongoing father–adult child relationships have implications for the ways in which new fathers seek to develop their roles (Brannen and Nilsen, 2006; Stelle and Sheehan, 2011). While many aspects of fathers' post-birth experience remain unstudied, literature reviews reveal that some have received more research attention in recent years. In particular, research has included cross-generational and longitudinal studies and what can be categorised as studies of fatherhood in adverse or less favourable circumstances. Of relevance to the focus of this chapter, this list also includes early postnatal experiences of fathers, particularly first-time fathers, and fatherhood in neonatal units.

Fathers encountering the normal early postnatal period

For some considerable time fathers have routinely been present in delivery rooms, although this situation is not evident to the same degree in postnatal settings. There are many reasons for this; some might be related to the mother's own situation. In the past, childbirth moved from home to a hospital setting and mothers spent prolonged periods of time separated from their newborns. During this time fathers were viewed as little more than disruptive visitors who interrupted the smooth and efficient conduct of hospital activities. This system of organising postnatal care provided few opportunities for mothers, and particularly fathers, to become acquainted with their baby. Later, as the concept of rooming in gained credence, and mother and baby were kept together where possible, fathers often continued to be seen as less important. This state of affairs might have contributed to fathers' feelings of marginalisation, dissatisfaction and estrangement from family life

(Finnbogadóttir et al, 2003; Deave and Johnson, 2008; Hildingsson et al, 2009; Steen et al, 2011).

Based upon research about what women wanted, and evidence about the benefits of reduced hospital stay, recent years have witnessed considerable changes in midwifery practice and routine postnatal care (National Institute for Health and Clinical Excellence, 2006). For example, initiatives to promote breastfeeding as the norm for mothers, and greater attempts to include fathers are increasingly evident. As a result, fathers are now more generally welcomed in postnatal settings, and services are striving to be more inclusive (Royal College of Midwives, 2012). Some of the changes relating to how fathers are engaged and involved reflect different ideas about the scope and nature of midwifery practice. However, research findings also underscore the benefits for mothers and children from fathers' early and continued presence in family life. Nonetheless, barriers to greater involvement of fathers in postnatal care remain, particularly in hospital settings, and many fathers can still feel unwelcome (Steen et al, 2011). Fathers say that one of the barriers to their greater involvement in hospital postnatal settings is that the predominantly female environment is intimidating and off-putting and this can reinforce their perception that their needs are secondary. To address this, the Royal College of Midwives has highlighted as exemplars of good practice the efforts of some maternity services to be more father inclusive in the way they organise and deliver their services (Royal College of Midwives, 2012).

Thomas et al (2011) found that first-time fathers and those with financial worries were particularly likely to perceive that they lacked support from midwives and their partner. Others have drawn attention to how some groups of fathers experience censure and anticipate prejudice from healthcare professionals which will affect their understanding of any support (Williams, 2007; Reeves and Rehal, 2008; Department of Health, 2010). A recent study in Finland (Oommen et al, 2011) included questionnaires administered to a sample of 500 fathers and concluded that both first-time and subsequent fathers desired greater social support from healthcare professionals. One way to provide increased levels of support for fathers can be through organising maternity services to ensure continuity of healthcare personnel. Aune et al (2011) detail the benefits of providing continuity of carer throughout pregnancy and into the postnatal period. In essence, a familiar face enables mothers and fathers to establish a trusting relationship with healthcare professionals and this has a positive impact on their level of satisfaction. Ensuring continuity seems to be a strategy to advocate for. Whatever the source of fathers' disquiet with their early postnatal experiences, it seems that more research into their needs around this time is required.

Some of the difficulty fathers face in the early postnatal period, principally in hospital settings, might reflect a lack of a clearly defined role. Some recent guidance has sought to formalise and increase the role of fathers in postnatal settings, journalistically reported as: 'New dads urged to muck in on maternity ward' (Templeton, 2011: 7). Although achieving benefits for mothers and children through fathers' early engagement is undoubtedly one objective, it also seems that reducing midwifery workload and responding to national shortages of midwives is a significant driver. However, this proposal is unlikely to either reduce the demand upon midwifery time in any meaningful way or facilitate greater father involvement. Presently, many mothers who receive healthcare professional support after birth complain that they still feel unprepared to care for their baby (Ellberg et al, 2010). The drive to involve fathers could lead to increased demands on midwifery time as most, particularly first-time fathers, without adequate preparation and support, would lack the ability to provide the level of mother and baby care expected. Some thought about the content and utility of existing programmes of fatherhood preparation is required to realise this proposal. Furthermore, this initiative is not without its problems; some midwives voice concern about the effect on mothers of an increased presence of men, citing issues of cultural sensitivity, domestic violence and distractions from focusing upon women's needs, and these anxieties need to be addressed.

Father involvement in the postnatal period

Cultural guidelines about what being a 'good' father involves are constantly shifting. Currently, the message conveyed is that involvement is the key attribute of a good father. When asked, many men state their intention to be more involved (Dermott, 2003; Henwood and Procter, 2003; O'Brien, 2005). Such declarations seem to be an enduring feature of contemporary fatherhood aspiration. Indeed recent figures suggest that around 25% of families with children say that childcare is shared equally between both (often working) parents (AVIVA, 2011). Furthermore, the number of fathers identified in the UK as the child's main carer has risen tenfold over the last decade and now accounts for 14% of all families (King, 2011). However, many fathers' contributions continue to be viewed as less important than those of mothers (Wall and Arnold, 2007).

The nature of involvement is inconsistently interpreted and numerous ideas about what involved fatherhood means feature in popular depictions of fatherhood. This situation is not confined to the UK and is seen across Europe (Gregory and Milner, 2011). Fathers are constantly exposed to ideas about what fatherhood entails from the media, their partners and friends, although how influential healthcare professionals are is seldom stated; this is an area that could be developed. Some of the difficulty with ideas about involved fatherhood is that the term lacks clarity (Wall and Arnold, 2007). One study established that young fathers identified several key characteristics of a good father under the umbrella of assuming responsibility. Specifically, this included being available, providing financial and emotional support for their children, and teaching their children moral standards of behaviour (Lemay et al, 2010). Another study of non-resident fathers found that many felt they were involved in their children's lives by virtue of being available for them should the need arise. Whilst some sought opportunities to interact with their children, others took a more passive role waiting for the child's mother to initiate contact (Forste et al, 2009). Despite their differences, both these studies are supportive of Lamb (1998) who suggests that father involvement can be considered in three domains: engagement, accessibility and responsibility. However, the relative intensity and balance between these three areas varies between fathers and across time, and further longitudinal study with fathers in different situations would be worthwhile.

There are two extreme interpretations of father involvement. In one, it is seen as being physically present in the family home (i.e. cohabiting with his children's mother) but not necessarily being involved in other provision or support for family life; a situation that LaRosa (1994) has referred to as, technically present but functionally absent. In the other interpretation, involvement is viewed as the father being a quasi mother, taking on increasing elements of childcare and home responsibilities. These highly polarised views are unhelpful as for most men involvement lies between these two extremes and invariably changes over time. Alternative ideas about involved fatherhood suggest it is less about redistributing childcare responsibilities, and instead more about fathers' motivations and behaviours that generate a greater commitment by them to their children and family life, in a way not previously expressed. However, most of the research concerning how involved fathering is practised in fathers' everyday lives is limited to studies about predominately white middle class men (Finn and Henwood, 2009). Consequently, generalisations to fatherhood in other contexts and circumstances should be treated with caution.

Research over many years on father–infant interactions in early childhood suggests that fathers devote more time to play and less to childcare when compared to mothers (Rustia and Abbott, 1993; Grossman et al, 1999; Tamis-LeMonda et al, 2004; O'Brien, 2005). This behaviour is conjectured as helping to prepare children for life outside the home and family (Thomas et al, 2011) and it seems to be important in masculine constructions of childcare (Easterbrooks and Goldberg, 1984; Brandth and Kvande, 1998). If correct, this style of parenting could help to distinguish fathers' childcare as distinct from and yet synergistic with that of mothers, and could mark a counterbalance to using maternal activities alone as the standard reference of childcare. Such invigorating parent–child interaction might be less appropriate during the time shortly after birth and this could help explain fathers' lack of visibility in childcare activities during this time.

Debate around father involvement reveals complex social processes at work. Existing models of fatherhood are built upon biological and ideological frames of reference. Many fathers are intuitively aware of aspects of these competing paradigms and many seek to include features of these models into their behaviours. It could be important when seeking to support fathers to understand why they adopt a particular style of fathering. In a large longitudinal study, Rustia and Abbott (1993) contrasted 122 men's normative expectations with their experiences of childcare in an attempt to predict fathering style. They concluded that fathers' participation in childcare was influenced by many factors, including self-esteem, birth experiences, the mother's education and employment status, and men's own childhood experiences. Cabrera et al (2000) add support, suggesting that what motivates men to adopt particular fathering styles is rooted in their childhood experiences with their own fathers, other family members and wider societal influences on gender role/identity development. More recently, Williams (2008) has argued that men's ideas about fatherhood are increasingly individualised as they respond to situational circumstances in their lives. If this is the case, then for most fathers, fathering behaviour has more to do with personal biography and social circumstances than philosophical adherence to any particular fatherhood style.

Fatherhood, family life and work

Becoming a father impacts upon existing roles in ways that many fathers initially fail to realise. While the amount of time spent in family activities has increased considerably since the 1970s (O'Brien, 2005), becoming more involved in family life can create tensions for fathers. After the birth of their first child family responsibilities begin to shape how many men think about their career (Ranson, 2001). In particular, enduring anxieties revolve around achieving a balance between work and family life (Ranson, 2001; Henwood and Procter, 2003; Smeaton, 2006; Equal Opportunities Commission, 2006, 2007; Gregory and Milner, 2011). However, evidence that fathers' increased family time has led to similar increases in their contributions to childcare and domestic labour is contradictory, and equitable divisions continue to elude most families (Yaxley et al, 2005). Some of this imbalance might arise from men's work, although even when both parents work outside the home, mothers often continue to provide disproportionate amounts of childcare and domestic work (Hochschild, 1994; Sullivan, 2000; Strazdins et al, 2004).

Following childbirth, many fathers' working hours tend to increase (O'Brien and Shemilt, 2003). This could be due to a number of reasons, for example, compensation for the loss of dual income, bearing increased family expenditure, or career progression (O'Brien and Shemilt, 2003). Whilst a causal relationship between longer working hours and fatherhood is a tempting interpretation, Dermott (2006) cautions against this, suggesting that often fatherhood just happens to coincide with a period in men's working lives that can necessitate longer working hours. Unsurprisingly, research into fathers' working hours has highlighted that working more than 50 hours per week has a detrimental effect on family life, particularly in terms of joint activities (Ferri and Smith, 1996; O'Brien and Shemilt, 2003).

Resolving tensions over income generation versus childcare responsibilities has become an element of family life for large numbers of UK families. Recent decades have witnessed a shift away from single income households, with increasing numbers of families now relying on dual incomes where both parents regularly work outside the home. This situation can often involve at least one parent working non-standard hours (Strazdins et al, 2004). However, in the UK, even when both parents earn, men tend to contribute the larger income (Johnson and Semmence, 2006). After childbirth, this income imbalance often becomes more marked (Dermott, 2006), although a recent survey suggests that in a small but increasing number of families it is mothers who remain the main income earner and fathers who reduce their paid working hours to become the main carer of their children (AVIVA, 2011). Such financial factors might pragmatically determine who takes on primary childcare responsibilities.

Despite increased expectations that fathers will be involved in childcare, until relatively recently men were not readily provided opportunities to do so. Lack of access to meaningful paternity leave, employment practices and economic circumstances reinforce existing gender divisions in many families (Thompson et al, 2005; Equal Opportunities Commission, 2006; Smeaton and Marsh, 2006). Regardless of a policy agenda that seeks to promote father involvement, some fathers continue to be seemingly comfortable on the sidelines of family life, engaging preferentially in the traditional role of 'provider' and 'breadwinner'. However, this could be seen as a way for them to express their involvement

(Christiansen and Palkovitz, 2001). Warin et al (1999), studying families with older children, suggest that this situation is attractive to some men as it affords higher status and simultaneously provides a legitimate channel to express their fatherhood responsibilities but is less emotionally demanding. Indeed fathers who seek to integrate 'family provider' and 'involved father' roles within their parental identity are more likely to report conflict when trying to reconcile these often contradictory expectations (Warin et al, 1999; Strazdins et al, 2004; Burgess, 2007). Clearly, for many men, integrating their ideas about involved fatherhood into their pre-existing perspectives on masculinity, work and family life is more complex and problematic than initial interpretations might suppose.

Mothers' gatekeeping

Fathers' roles in families are dynamic and cannot be isolated from other aspects of men's lives; they are simultaneously embedded in and constrained by culturally defined parameters (Woollett and Nicolson, 1998; Steinberg and Kruckman, 2000). Some factors, such as the demands of work, statute, official policy and cultural change, that have influenced and driven changes in men's fathering behaviours, have been outlined. However, there is one highly important and powerful source of influence over fathers that has not been considered, that of mothers themselves. The attitudes of mothers towards fathers can be influential in determining whether or not fathers get involved, and the level of that involvement (Beital and Parke, 1998). Some mothers can find it difficult to accept men's involvement with their children, seeing it as an invasion of their sphere of parenting territory (Henderson and Brouse, 1991). Concern that mothers might, in some situations, seek to limit men's participation in childcare is conceptualised as 'maternal gatekeeping' (Allen and Hawkins, 1999). Maternal gatekeeping represents a collection of beliefs and behaviours about what fathers should and can do. These ideas can have a significant influence upon fatherhood behaviours (Kraemer, 1995; Fagan and Barnett, 2003; McBride et al, 2005; Yaxley et al, 2005).

Notions of such explicit expressions of maternal power within the family are seemingly incongruous, with much of the debate concerning men's powerful positions within society (Connell, 1987; Segal, 1997; Hearn, 2004) and the literature relating to how men influence mothers' decisions (Earle, 2000; Pontes et al, 2008; Sweet and Darbyshire, 2009; Bedwell et al, 2011). Nevertheless, Backett (1987) asserts that mothers hold considerable, although often covert, power within the family, particularly in relation to child rearing decisions. How this power is exerted to influence fathers' behaviour is not entirely clear.

One longitudinal study of 90 couples sought to identify behaviours that constituted gatekeeping in two parent contexts and to assess their effect. Analysis of data from a pre-existing survey concerning beliefs about roles and parental regulation suggest a correlation between mothers being less critical and offering more encouragement to fathers and the latter's greater relative involvement (Schoppe-Sullivan et al, 2008). A recent study of fathers in a neonatal unit corroborates this finding. Observational fieldwork data illustrate that when mothers are verbally supportive of their partner's involvement they often sought out opportunities to involve them. For example, one mother of a preterm baby discussing with a neonatal nurse when next to feed her baby said, 'I will save the next bottle feed for the evening when her dad will be visiting so he can do it'. Another, discussing bathing her baby, said, 'I'll leave it [baby bath] till tonight when his dad is here, otherwise he's missing out' (Hugill, 2009: 178). Whilst these mothers were promoting involvement rather than seeking to limit it, they were nonetheless continuing to define the parameters of father involvement. The reality of what determines fathers' behaviours in individual families is complex; mothers' ideas and beliefs are clearly one of a number of sources of influence that shape father involvement. Healthcare professionals can help support fathers' involvement by discussing with mothers their attitudes towards involving the father of their baby.

Beneficial effects of father involvement

In contrast to past generations, the current view is that fathers should be more involved with maternity care and their children's lives, and this is a widely held opinion. There is an accumulating body of evidence about the beneficial effects that involving fathers in maternity care and family life has upon their own, their partner's and their children's health, development and wellbeing. Despite some men posing a risk to their partners and children, recent extensive reviews of the research concerning the effects of fathers' contributions to family life (Allen et al, 2007; Flouri, 2005; Burgess, 2008) argue that the weight of evidence for promoting and facilitating father involvement in family life and the lives of their children is unassailable.

Effects of father involvement on mothers and children

Contrary to ideas that fathers are of peripheral importance, the quantity and quality of their contributions has direct and indirect effects upon their children's development and wellbeing, and these can be far reaching. One research study showed that fathers who provided skin-to-skin care for their baby shortly after caesarean section birth were able calm their baby, reduce crying and facilitate pre-feeding behaviours in a way similar to mothers (Erlandsson et al, 2007). However, Dermott (2003, 2008) asserts that much of the importance of fathers' involvement lies beyond their contributions to direct childcare or gender role-modelling and instead derive from a father's individual emotional connectedness with his children. Numerous research studies have sought to examine and quantify the effects of father involvement and Allen et al (2007) and Burgess (2008) bring together useful reviews of much of this body of research. In essence, the effects of positive father involvement can be summarised across a range of measures relating to physical and mental health, educational attainment and socialisation.

A recent systemic review of 16 longitudinal studies (24 papers) on the effects of fathers' involvement on children's developmental outcomes concluded that active and regular engagement by fathers with their children can predict a range of positive outcomes, particularly for disadvantaged groups (Sarkadi et al, 2008). Early father involvement shows positive correlations with educational accomplishment, such as increased cognitive ability at the ages of six and 12 months and higher IQ by the age of three (Allen et al, 2007), and can predict higher academic achievement by the age of 20 years (Flouri and Buchanan, 2004), especially in boys. However, typically, fathers in many of these studies were in general more educated and more likely to be employed and living with their partner, so generalisations should be treated with caution. Rowe et al (2004) suggest that one mechanism to explain this effect might arise from the way fathers talk to their children. From early on fathers tend to use speech characteristics such as asking 'What' and 'Why', questions that require a more thoughtful response and ultimately aid children to develop a wider vocabulary. When mothers see fathers behaving this way with their children they incorporate similar behaviours into their play (Tamis-LeMonda et al, 2004). This potentially synergistic effect might be important, but further research is required.

There are also correlations between fathers' involvement and reductions in the likelihood of childhood health-related problems, such as obesity and depression (Flouri and Buchanan, 2003; Flouri, 2005). Other areas, including greater sociability (reduced drug misuse, antisocial behaviour, criminality), increased moral responsibility (tolerance and concern for others), and happiness also feature (Flouri, 2005; Allen et al, 2007). Some of the effects are different for boys and girls, for example, father involvement reduces behavioural problems in boys but in girls involvement is associated with reduced psychological morbidity in adolescence (Sarkadi et al, 2008). Inevitably, effects change over time and the exact mechanisms are unclear. It is possible that increased emotional attachment to the father and higher self-esteem, together with indirect effects, such as facilitating optimum health in mothers, might be factors.

Fathers are also known to affect the health and wellbeing of mothers in positive and negative ways. For example, parental smoking is known to have significant health effects on children both before and after birth (Button et al, 2007; Jauniaux and Greenough, 2007; Ekbald et al, 2010). Around pregnancy and birth many mothers try to stop smoking for their own and their child's health. Fathers can be instrumental in supporting mothers to stop smoking or place considerable obstacles that dissuade them from quitting (Burgess, 2008).

When fathers are prepared for their role during labour and are actively engaged during this time, mothers (and fathers) report more positive feelings regarding the labour, and experience fewer problems (Wöckel et al, 2007). Mothers are also more likely to continue with breastfeeding (Datta et al, 2012). However, in reality the extent and form of support that mothers' can anticipate differs across socioeconomic and cultural boundaries. It is important for healthcare professionals to be aware of culturally mediated gender dynamics as mothers' and fathers' experiences, and health and wellbeing are interdependent. Measures that aim to improve men's understanding of their family and social roles and the effects that their behaviours can have upon the health and wellbeing of their partner and children are to be welcomed.

For some families, when mothers are suffering from postnatal depression fathers' involvement is reported to have a compensatory effect on their children's welfare (Mezulis et al, 2004). Conversely, partners of depressed women can have less positive interactions with their children and their behaviours can exacerbate the effects of maternal depression (Mezulis et al, 2004; Goodman, 2008). In addition they are more likely to become depressed themselves, with several studies reporting a correlation between postnatal depression in mothers and depression in fathers (Paulson and Bazemore, 2010; Wilson and Durbin, 2010). Depressed fathers can have enduring and harmful effects on their children's early behavioural and emotional development (Ramchandani et al, 2005; Wilson and Durbin, 2010). Fathers' own depression seems to affect children differently to depression in mothers but the situation is unclear and requires further research.

Effects of father involvement on the father himself

Fathers' experiences during the antenatal period and events around birth can be influential on their postnatal emotional wellbeing, sense of affinity with their family and their readiness to engage in child caring activities (Greenhalgh et al, 2000; Persson et al, 2007). Key external factors affecting fathers' readiness include the empowering behaviours of healthcare practitioners and their sense of their partner's wellbeing (Persson et al, 2007). These factors might have implications for fathers in situations where they are the child's primary carer, where their partner is ill or where they lack access to support or others fail to sanction their involvement.

For a man, becoming a father can have wide-ranging effects on his physical and psychological health. Perhaps the most important benefit is that fatherhood affords a legitimate opportunity to display affection and emotion. Ferketich and Mercer (1995) have suggested that becoming a father and getting involved in childcare can increase men's feelings of attachment to their children and increase their level of social connectivity with others, which can boost self-esteem and mental wellbeing. In the short term for up to year after birth fatherhood, particularly for first-time fathers, is associated with increased stress and poorer health and mental wellbeing (Bartlett, 2004). Some of this might be related to the emotional upheavals and adjustments to fatherhood. Conversely, in the long term some evidence suggests that becoming a father is advantageous to men's physical and psychological wellbeing and longevity (Bartlett, 2004). Why this should be so is the subject of some debate. Longitudinal studies of the effects of fatherhood on health are few. However, one study, a retrospective analysis of cardiac disease in older men, found that men with two or more children had a significantly lower lifetime risk of coronary heart disease than men with fewer children or who were never fathers (Lawlor et al, 2003). Such relationships should be treated with caution as some of the health effects attributed to fatherhood might be due to other lifestyle confounders such as marital status, employment and life-long changes in diet or levels of physical activity.

One area of men's health that has recently risen to prominence after many years of failing to be recognised is paternal postpartum depression. It now seems that this is a real phenomenon associated with the postpartum period, rather than just a circumstantial timing of depressive symptoms. A recent meta-analysis of over 40 studies (Paulson and Bazemore, 2010) highlighted that during pregnancy and for up to one year post-birth the frequency of self-reported depression in fathers was twice that seen in the wider male population, although there is considerable international variation. While preterm birth is know to be a factor affecting mothers' mental health (Holditch-Davis et al, 2003; Ringland, 2008), it is less clear for fathers. It is likely that our current understanding of the prevalence of this disorder in fathers is incomplete. There are many possible reasons for under-reporting, including some diagnostic bias. Depression in men can be difficult to recognise as the symptoms can be different from those experienced by women, and traditional masculine norms of health-seeking behaviour can mean that fathers might be less likely than mothers to recognise their mental health needs and to seek help. Notwithstanding the limitations of some of the studies reviewed by Paulson and Bazemore (2010), there is clearly something happening to fathers' mental health status. Healthcare professionals involved in the care of mothers during pregnancy and infancy should familiarise themselves with the symptoms of depression in men and take an empathic whole-family approach to their mental wellbeing assessment and screening activities.

Fathers in neonatal units

In recent years the number of registered births in the UK has increased; in 2009 it was 706 000 and by 2010 this figure had increased to around 720 000 (Beaumont, 2011). Rates of preterm birth and admission to neonatal units vary across local, national and international boundaries but on average in the UK it affects approximately 1 in 10 of all births. This incidence means that whilst most pregnancies are unaffected over 70 000 families require access to a neonatal unit and their lives are affected by the consequences of this encounter. It can therefore be surmised that more and more fathers are encountering preterm birth.

The neonatal unit is a world apart from the more usual experience of early infancy. The interruption of pregnancy by preterm birth can bring about a deep crisis in families. Feelings of being ill prepared characterise many new fathers' thoughts and these are exaggerated in neonatal units. All the studies to date support the view that preterm birth is a stressful experience for parents (Aagaard and Hall, 2008; Sloan et al, 2008; Obeidat et al, 2009) and one that has enduring consequences for family wellbeing (Holditch-Davis et al, 2003; Ringland, 2008; Zelkowitz, et al, 2009; Tryvaud et al, 2011). Whilst a significant portion of this stress relates to the nature of the neonatal unit experience, Tryvaud et al (2011) highlight the contribution that pre-existing mental health symptoms can make to parental stress responses. Despite the broad consensus, there is limited agreement on the optimum choice of intervention to support parents during this time and mixed evidence regarding the usefulness of individual interventions. Most studies have focused on mothers and often sought to measure the intensity of stress experience or individual resilience and coping. The emerging challenge is to identify predictive factors that may indicate the need for increased support. In some studies there is evidence that mothers and fathers experience and respond to preterm birth differently (Doering et al, 1999; Carter et al, 2007; Feeley et al, 2007; Sloan et al, 2008; Kikkert et al, 2010). These gender differences persist, regardless of whether or not the health problem is neonatal in origin or arises later in childhood (Pelchat et al, 2007; Swallow et al, 2011).

Fathers' experiences and needs

Being a father on a neonatal unit can be extremely isolating. These fathers are faced with an unexpected emotional and worrisome situation in an environment with which they are unfamiliar and which those outside often fail to comprehend. For fathers, the experience of preterm birth can be significant and life altering. When asked, some fathers say that these experiences are more intense than previous fatherhood experience and as a result they feel more attached to this baby (Lindberg et al, 2008; Hugill, 2009). While it is usual for new fathers to experience emotional discomfort and periods of anxiety, fathers who have a preterm baby face additional stressors. Reconciling the sometimes contradictory emotions of joy and worry over the birth can pose particular difficulties. One interview study of fathers' experiences identified a number of aspects. These included positive feelings about becoming a father but at the same time concern about their baby and partner mixed with feelings of helplessness. In addition they felt stress relating to difficulties in prioritising roles of husband, father, and family wage earner (Lundqvist and Jakobsson, 2003).

Many fathers in neonatal units frame their ideas about involved fatherhood as relating to all their activities, including work, as being supportive of family life and greater involvement with their children (Pohlman, 2005; Lindberg et al, 2007). This reflects the situation seen elsewhere (Christiansen and Palkovitz, 2001) but sometimes work can become the dominant focus (Pohlman, 2005) and could reflect a desire by fathers to distance themselves from emotionally upsetting circumstances. Fathers reporting tensions over balancing time with their baby and partner with wider responsibilities is a recurring feature in neonatal fatherhood research. However, this is not unique to fatherhood in neonatal units; following childbirth many fathers in other circumstances express similar difficulties (St John et al, 2004; Fägerskiöld, 2008; Persson et al, 2011).

Some research reports that fathers often act as a communication conduit between healthcare professionals, their partner and other family members (Locock and Alexander, 2006). This situation is also seen during difficult birth, neonatal resuscitation and following admission to a neonatal unit (Lindberg et al, 2007; Harvey, 2010). However, there is some evidence of an additional component; fathers often censor information seemingly to provide an emotional buffer and protect their partner's psychological health. This behaviour comes with an emotional cost, as one father recalls, 'There were things that I didn't tell her [partner]. Like he [baby] was having an operation [umbilical line insertion]. I was telling her all the good things, I was trying to protect her, I know I shouldn't have' (Hugill, 2009: 200). For a number of fathers their primary role during this time is to protect their partners from further emotional harm (Lee et al, 2005) and 'play the strong one and hold it all together' (Hugill, 2009: 202). However, such behaviour betrays one of the 'myths of manhood' that men do not have needs of their own because they are strong (Seidler, 2007). This behaviour could lead to adverse psychological outcomes, and healthcare professionals should be mindful of this risk.

Lundqvist and colleagues (2007) characterised fathers' experiences as a process during which they move from detachment toward closeness to their baby as they establish attachments. Many fathers in more usual postnatal contexts feel they occupy an indeterminate state between father and visitor with no established role, and feel relegated to the margins (Steen et al, 2011). One survey found that this sense of marginalisation was replicated in neonatal units: 'It would have been easy to be a visitor rather than a dad' (POPPY Steering Group, 2009: 10). A Canadian study using interviews with fathers whose baby had spent time on a neonatal unit highlighted an additional source of stress; they sensed a loss of control over events (Arockiasamy et al, 2007). This loss of control, although only partially related to emotional control, represents another facet of some men's ideas about normative masculine behaviour (Connell, 2005). Healthcare professionals can help fathers gain a level of control by providing them with information about preterm babies, by suggesting ways in which they can be supportive to their partner and baby's recovery and involving them in decision making about everyday matters.

Clearly, supporting fathers' needs for information and communication could help reduce their overall stress. Spence and Lau (2006) characterise the culture of neonatal units as one that embraces consensual decision-making although this is not universal. Whilst staff-led information provision to parents is widely seen, in one study fathers who were self-confident in seeking information were viewed as potentially threatening and their behaviour was less welcomed (Hugill, 2009). Independent health information seeking is known to contribute to individual empowerment (the expert patient, for example); healthcare professionals, rather than censuring fathers, could more actively facilitate information seeking which would further enable them to establish feelings of control and influence over events and decisions affecting their baby.

However, the evidence regarding fathers' experiences in neonatal units is not straightforward. Despite methodological, cultural and geographical differences, studies of fathers in neonatal units have some consistencies. These include fathers' concern for the wellbeing of their baby and partner, fear of losing control over events and their emotions, and feelings of vulnerability. Together, these increase fathers' stress experience.

Emotional impacts

For most fathers, during their partner's pregnancy, the possibility of admission to a neonatal unit does not feature in their thoughts. Consequently, the overwhelming response of most fathers at the time of admission is one of acute and often severe emotional shock which results in feelings of disconnection from everyday life (Harvey, 2010). In this, their emotional reactions are very similar to mothers, although they are coloured by individual fathers' ideas about appropriate masculine emotional responses. Nonetheless, there is certainly a need for emotionally supportive behaviours to be directed towards fathers, although these are sometimes constrained by concern over their suitability, as one nurse recalled (Hugill, 2009: 224): 'The relationship with fathers is different to that with mothers. Touch is often used with mothers as [a] comfort measure; [it] may not feel appropriate with fathers.'

Increasingly, emotional openness is becoming associated with ideas about what is involved in being a good father (Dermott, 2008). However, emotional experiences are inherently subjective and their study continues to generate considerable debate (Theodosisus, 2006). Burkitt (1997) argues that sharing emotions or suppressing emotional expression can have important social functions. Consequently, questions about how fathers control their emotions and which emotional displays are condoned are integral to our understanding of their experiences. Starting fatherhood in a neonatal unit can result in fathers' witnessing emotionally distressing events. At first, fathers often lack social knowledge about acceptable emotional behaviours, what Hochschild (1979) refers to as 'feeling rules'. For some fathers the first sight of their baby on the neonatal unit can create overwhelming emotions that their previous experiences have not equipped them to deal with. This can for some men be more upsetting than their anxieties about their baby and partner.

In distressing circumstances some fathers fall back upon previously learnt behaviours or adopt stereotypical masculine guises, such as suppressing their emotional expression, or showing bravado or anger, seemingly to protect themselves from emotional peril (Duncombe and Marsden, 1998, 1999; Seidler, 2007). This behaviour enables them in part to 'switch off' problematic and distressing stimuli and distance themselves from stressful circumstances. Fathers often expend considerable effort managing their emotions in front of others and often seek out private or emotionally secure spaces before revealing how they feel (Hugill, 2009; Harvey, 2010). These behaviours are entirely in keeping with dominant concepts of masculinity which continue to define men as independent and self-sufficient, leaving little opportunity for recognising emotional needs (Seidler, 2007). In addition, Kim (2009) argues that in some cultures sharing emotions verbally can suggest interpersonal trust and intimacy; this might be lacking in the early period after admission and make some men uncomfortable with expressing their emotions in front of neonatal unit staff.

In these circumstances, seeking out ways to offer fathers additional male friendly information, such as *Facts for fathers* (Bliss, 2010), and social support, perhaps through increasing the visibility of male workers or engaging fathers in social talk and enquiring into their welfare and feelings, might be beneficial in making fathers feel more emotionally secure. Because men tend to express emotions differently from women it is important to avoid mistaking their emotional control as ambivalence, disinterest or that they are not experiencing emotional upheaval. Indeed, because fathers often deal with their emotions in solitary ways they might be more vulnerable than mothers during intensely stressful situations.

Strategies to engage and involve fathers

Fathers who are highly motivated and confident are able to negotiate their roles with ease. However, less confident or motivated fathers can find it harder to overcome barriers to their greater involvement (Fatherhood Institute, 2011). It is to this latter group of fathers that strategies to promote greater involvement can be most successful. Contrary to ideas that fathers have greater choice in their family roles, mothers are known are to be highly influential and their attitudes can influence the degree of father involvement. Consequently any interventions delivered by healthcare professionals with the aim of encouraging greater paternal involvement should also include some exploration of mothers' underlying attitudes towards fathers' involvement.

Many strategies aimed at increasing fathers' involvement, in general and in neonatal units, cut across pregnancy, birth and early infancy. In the previous chapter we considered some of the approaches to connect with fathers during adverse events; these are relevant here and we will not restate them, but the widely distributed publication, *Including new fathers: A guide for maternity professionals* (Fatherhood Institute, 2007) provides a useful summation of key ways to increase engagement with fathers during pregnancy, birth and afterwards. In this section we draw attention to some additional strategies that healthcare professionals can use to enhance fathers' involvement and commitment.

Factors that are known to affect parents' sense of security and satisfaction in the postnatal period include a sense of autonomy, midwives' and nurses' support and empowering behaviours, and the quality of the relationship within the family (Persson et al, 2007; Hildingsson et al, 2009). For fathers, feelings around being treated considerately, having a sense of participation and being noticed seem to be important factors in determining their satisfaction (Persson et al, 2007, 2011; Ellberg et al, 2008; Hildingsson et al, 2009). Previously, we have emphasised the need to provide private spaces which fathers can use to find solace or stay overnight; this is recognised in several policy and standards publications (Bliss, 2009; Department of Health, 2009; Royal College of Midwives, 2012). However, there is considerable variability in the recognition of this need and its availability, and managers should advocate on behalf of fathers for this provision. The recent report from the Royal College of Midwives (2012: 11) drew attention to the efforts several hospitals had made to help fathers to stay with their partner and newborn baby to encourage attachments to form, to support their partners and to 'be a visible parent'. However, healthcare professionals need to be fully cognisant with family circumstances as there will be situations when this might not be in the father's, mother's or baby's best interests.

During the first few days and weeks of new parenthood most parents strive to learn about caring for their baby. Healthcare professionals are ideally placed to be highly influential in this process. In the UK, most maternity and neonatal units and a number of other organisations provide a range of antenatal and postnatal activities that aim to prepare and support parents in gaining parenting skills. There is a concern that some of these interventions might be perceived as dictating particular preferred parenting styles or lack cultural sensitivity, and evidence about the benefits for mothers and fathers is ambiguous. According to several systematic reviews, there is a lack of robust empirical evidence to support the effectiveness of parenthood educational programmes in equipping parents with the skills to care for their newborn children (Gagnon and Sandall, 2007; Bryanton and Beck, 2010). Nevertheless, when targeted interventions reach out to specific sub-groups of parents or are aimed at changing particular types of parenting behaviour then the outcomes seem to be more effective (Kaarensen et al, 2006; Magill-Evans et al, 2006; Turan et al, 2008; Fatherhood Institute, 2009, 2011; Royal College of Midwives, 2012).

Bayley et al (2009) identify some of the barriers discouraging fathers from participating in parenthood education. Although some fathers deliberately avoid officialdom, fearing criticism and discrimination, much of the culpability for fathers' failure to access such services arises from systemic organisational shortcomings. This can leave fathers isolated from potential sources of support and advice. Barriers include failing to publicise services in places where men will see it, poor timing around competing commitments, such as work, and perceptions that services are solely focused towards mothers. Some thought around the imagery and language used in advertising and delivering interventions will go some way to removing these barriers. Moreover, organisations that lack detailed local interpretations of national policies that promote father inclusion or view fathers as presenting a series of problems requiring resolution pose particularly intransigent obstacles. Healthcare professionals need to appreciate how their own attitudes and behaviours can erode or reinforce these obstructions. In addition, it is essential that there is an awareness of the barriers, both local and in general, that limit fathers' involvement and ways to overcome these.

While the development of clearly articulated polices with rationales and targets has an important contribution to make (Fatherhood Institute, 2007), it is often the little things that can make a difference and help fathers feel more welcome (Royal College of Midwives, 2012). Providing a forum where healthcare professionals can reflect upon and challenge attitudes towards fathers' roles might be worth considering, particularly if a number of staff are ambivalent or have provocative opinions about the benefits of involving fathers. While healthcare professionals receive training in communication, equipping them with the additional necessary skills and language to communicate usefully with fathers can positively affect mothers' and fathers' satisfaction (Fatherhood Institute, 2009; Weiss et al, 2010). Effective communication, mutual respect and collaborative decision making are all important hallmarks of family-centred care (Hutchfield, 1999). As such, training about fathers and their needs should be routinely included in professional development and pre-registration education and could make important contributions to making care truly family-centred.

There is also some evidence that providing support and training for fathers on their own can enhance the birth experience for both partners (Wöckel et al, 2007), but there is some concern about focusing upon one parent in isolation (Bayley et al, 2009). When asked, many fathers would like to attend a postnatal parenting class with their baby (Matthey and Barnett, 1999), and whilst not all men will want this it is important they have the opportunity to do so. Any programme recommended should have proven positive effects on parenting ability. Initiatives that provide physical and emotional spaces that legitimatise men to express their fears and talk about their psychological responses to pregnancy and fatherhood show promise and should be considered as one of a range of ways to promote greater support for fathers.

Ideas about parental support are embedded in many neonatal units; however, the term is open to a variety of interpretations. One refers to interventions that seek to reduce parents' stress response whilst others focus on improving parenting style. Evaluations of programmes seeking to reduce stress have mixed results

(Kaarensen et al, 2006; Turan et al, 2008). Nevertheless those that focus upon providing social support and educational information about preterm infants and their care seem to be well received by parents and warrant further development to tailor them to individual parent needs. The inclusion of content about preterm development and understanding baby behaviour might be worthwhile.

Parents view good communication from healthcare professionals as supportive of their involvement with their baby's care. However, it is not always evident (Cone, 2007; Lam et al, 2007). When asked, parents place particular value upon receiving emotional support, guidance on baby care and consistency and clarity of communication from those involved in looking after their baby (POPPY Steering Group, 2009). The POPPY report (POPPY Steering Group, 2009) emphasises the continued existence of gaps, particularly in relation to parent support and information and communication needs. A recent national postal survey of parents' experiences of neonatal services reported that whilst most parents had a largely positive experience there were wide variations between units (Howell and Graham, 2011). Participating units received an individual report which ranked them against the highest scoring units to help them prepare action plans to address any shortcomings. Questionnaires were mailed to mothers' addresses. It is unclear how responses from mothers and fathers were broken down and it is possible that most responses represent mothers' views or some negotiated compromise. In view of the evidence that mothers and fathers can have different perspectives on their neonatal experience this possible respondent gender bias needs considering in future surveys.

Communication between healthcare professionals and fathers can be a source of stress, confusion, dissatisfaction and, sometimes, conflict. Some of this might be due to differences in how fathers perceive and comprehend events and issues compared to others. Healthcare professionals can help overcome some of these problems by providing forums for consistent and meaningful communication. On neonatal units, Peticuff and Arbeart (2005) advocate the routine use of 'infant progress charts' and 'parent–professional planning meetings' as one way to ensure more effective inclusion and communication with parents. Others advocate including parents on ward rounds and providing more targeted information. On postnatal wards, the use of routine events, such as the formal newborn examination, could provide similar opportunities to involve and communicate with fathers. Appleton (2011) recommends that fathers are notified of the timing of this examination and that they are encouraged to attend since the examination provides an opportunity for them to learn about their baby and how to interpret his/her behaviours. All these interventions have merits and should be included in a cohesive and publicised father communication policy.

The early postnatal period provides an additional opportunity to promote father involvement and build upon his involvement during pregnancy and birth. However, its potential remains unrealised in most locations and it is salutary for healthcare professionals to look for ways to do this. One way this can be achieved is to carry out an evaluation and audit of current services, and those with managerial responsibilities should be encouraging and facilitative of such initiatives. The National Childbirth Trust (2012) advocates using a three-point check entitled *How father friendly are you?* This simple and easy to use tool poses a series of self-directed questions prompting users to reflect on their attitudes and the physical and social environment where father-directed services are delivered. It could be used by individual healthcare professionals or form the basis for wider service evaluation. For neonatal units, Bliss (2012) has recently launched an audit tool, called the *Bliss baby charter audit tool* to help units evaluate their compliance with existing standards (Bliss, 2009; Department of Health, 2009) and develop their service. Whilst targeted at neonatal services, the standards and assessment criteria are readily transferable to other postnatal settings. For those with wider managerial and service commissioning and evaluation remits in local trusts and networks the 10-point commissioning checklist from the Fatherhood Institute (2009) provides some clear evidence-based criteria for parenting programmes. These 10 points, covering areas such as organisational policy frameworks, embedding father-focused staff training and mechanisms to assess and meet fathers' needs, for example, could form the basis of either a commissioning or evaluation framework to drive for a more father-inclusive and family-centred service provision.

In summation there is no one best strategy to increase fathers' involvement and what works in one context may fail in another. There is a need to understand better the kinds of support that fathers want and need during this time and design services to deliver this support; whether this is at home on a hospital postnatal ward or neonatal unit. It would seem that there is scope for further research in this area. Perhaps one of the most effective techniques to engage with fathers is for individual healthcare professionals to talk with them on an emotional level and to ask them about how they feel about their experiences and about what they want and expect to do.

Conclusion

The benefits to mothers, their children and men themselves of involving fathers continue to be proven. Parent and baby interaction provides the foundations for establishing secure attachments with consequently better psychological, cognitive and emotional outcomes for children. The nature of this interaction in the early postnatal period is influenced by diverse factors including environmental context, individual behaviours, mental health status and sources of emotional support for both parents.

For fathers, much has changed; not long ago they had little place in postnatal care but now it is increasingly acknowledged that they have a key role to play in providing childcare and support for mothers. Involved fathering is an emerging ideology and pre-eminent within this concept is an assertion that good fathers should adopt a form of fathering that devotes more time to family. However, the evidence regarding what it means to be a good father tends to be more eclectic. Fatherhood is increasingly defined by its diversity rather than by its adherence to a limited range of stereotypical father types. Consequently, it might be better to refer to 'fatherhoods' in the plural to reflect the complexity and diversity of men's lives as fathers. Research on fathers' experiences has expanded in recent years but when compared with mothers, there remain considerable gaps in our understanding, and further longitudinal research into most aspects of fatherhood would be helpful to inform service design.

Key points

- Fathers, like mothers, need to develop their childcare skills in the postnatal period and services need to be structured in a way that offers them opportunities to do this
- The health information and support needs of fathers during the early postnatal period are inadequately considered
- Fathers with a baby in a neonatal unit experience additional sources of stress which share commonalties and differences with that seen with mothers in similar situations
- In neonatal units fathers' emotional responses are influenced by a complex interplay between their own perceptions and what they and others think is appropriate
- Healthcare professionals who are aware of how their own attitudes and beliefs about fathers and fatherhood affect the ways they relate to fathers seem better able to support fathers
- There is a need for more extensive research into most areas of fathers' postnatal and neonatal experiences to determine their expectations and needs during this time

---

Case history 1
A father in a postnatal ward

Ian's partner, Janice, has just had her second, but Ian's first baby. Ian feels that his own father 'wasn't much good' and that 'he doesn't want to look after his baby the way he was looked after by his dad'. He is determined to do the right things for his child. He is very keen to be involved in every aspect of his child's care and wants to stay on the postnatal ward with his partner so he can 'bond with and get to know his baby'. On this particular postnatal ward this is discouraged, but Ian insists and he stays.

Ian doesn't have much experience of dealing with babies and is constantly seeking out healthcare staff asking lots of questions about what are to them either trivial matters or not relevant at this point in time. This behaviour is viewed by some as merely annoying but by others as intimidating and controlling and as such it seemingly confirms their desire to resist the presence of fathers during this time. Ian sees it differently; no one seems to have any time for him and he is frustrated as everyone seems to tell him different things.

Reflective questions

- What factors might have led these members of the healthcare team to think about fathers in the ways they do and how are these opinions impacting upon the support they offer to fathers?
- What might be the effects of these points of view upon fathers' experiences?
- What additional resources could Ian have accessed for support and information at this time?
- What could healthcare professionals, Janice, and Ian himself have done to help prepare him for his postnatal role?
- What strategies could be implemented to challenge some of the opinions expressed about fathers that feature in this scenario in your practice area?

Case history 2
Emergency admission to a neonatal unit

Robert received a phone call at work telling him that his partner Sandra was about to have an emergency caesarean section for an obstetric emergency. He arrives at the hospital unaware that his third child, a daughter of 27 weeks' gestation, has been born and admitted to the neonatal unit. On arrival at the hospital he is uncertain what has happened or what to do. He is told he cannot see his partner because she is still in theatre; no one is able to give him an update on his partner's condition but they tell him that someone will speak with him later. Somebody suggest that whilst he is waiting, he could go to the neonatal unit and points the way. He leaves on his own in that direction. Once there he is met by a nurse who escorts him to incubator where his daughter is and begins to explain matters. On seeing his daughter intubated and attached to ventilator he becomes visibly pale and looks fearful. Worrying that he might faint, the nurse provides him with a chair and as he sits says: 'It's OK, it's just a bit hot in here.'

He does not listen properly to further explanation, and asks only about when his partner can visit. After regaining his composure he quietly leaves and seeks out the men's lavatory. Here he vomits and in a cubicle begins to cry quietly, quite overwhelmed by everything that has happen. His mobile rings, it is his partner's mother; he ignores it feeling unable to speak with her about what has happened. Some hours later he returns to his partner's bedside. He reveals nothing of his previous turmoil to Sandra telling himself that it would only upset her further and he has no wish to add to her worries and distress. Instead he talks about the baby and what he has seen on the neonatal unit in an upbeat manner before moving on to focus on everyday matters; buying milk on the way home and collecting their other children from school.

Reflective questions

- What factors might have led Robert to suppress and conceal his emotions from others?
- What might be the effects of this behaviour on Robert's health?
- To what extent do the experiences of Robert in this scenario reflect or counter your own experience of fathers in similarly difficult and worrying circumstances?
- How could delivery suite staff helped to prepare and support Robert for what

he saw and experienced in the neonatal unit?

- What could the healthcare team have done to support Robert after he left the neonatal unit? Which members of the healthcare team should take responsibility for doing this?
- What could the healthcare team do to support Sandra at this time to help to remove the responsibility that Robert felt to focus on her needs rather than his own or theirs? Again, which members of the healthcare team should take responsibility for doing this?

References

Aagaard H, Hall EOC (2008) Mothers' experiences of having a preterm infant in the neonatal care unit: A meta-synthesis. *Journal of Pediatric Nursing* **23**(3): e26–e36

Allen S, Daly K with Father Involvement Research Alliance (2007) *The effects of father involvement: An updated research summary of the evidence.* Centre for Families, Work and Well-Being, Guelph ON

Allen SM, Hawkins AJ (1999) Maternal gatekeeping: Mothers' beliefs and behaviours that inhibit greater father involvement in family work. *Journal of Marriage and the Family* **61**(1): 199–212

Appleton J (2011) Newborn behavioural aspects. In: Lomax A (ed) *Examination of the newborn.* Wiley Blackwell, Chichester

Arockiasamy V, Holsti L, Albersheim S (2007) Fathers' experiences in the neonatal intensive care unit: A search for control. *Pediatrics* **121**(2): e215–e222

Aune I, Dahlberg U, Ingebrigsten O (2011) Parents' experiences of midwifery students proving continuity of care. *Midwifery* doi:10.1016/j.midw.2011.06.006

AVIVA (2011) *Dads take on childcare duties in one in seven UK households.* Available from: http://www.aviva.co.uk/media-centre/story/14095/dads-take-on-childcare-duties-in-one-in seven-uk-h/ (accessed 23 January 2012)

Backett K (1987) The negotiation of fatherhood. In: Lewis C, O'Brien M (eds) *Reassessing fatherhood: New observations on fathers and the modern family.* Sage, London

Bartlett EE (2004) The effects of fatherhood on the health of men: A review of the literature. *Journal of Men's Health and Gender* **1**(2–3): 159–69

Bayley J, Wallace LM, Choudhry K (2009) Fathers and parenting programmes: Barriers and best practice. *Community Practitioner* **82**(4): 28–31

Beaumont J (ed) (2011) *Households and families. Social Trends 41.* Office for National Statistics, London

Bedwell C, Houghton G, Richens Y, Lavender T (2011) 'She can choose, as long as I'm happy with it': A qualitative study of expectant fathers' views on birth place. *Sexual and Reproductive Healthcare* **2**: 71–5

Beitel AH, Parke RD (1998) Paternal involvement in infancy: The role of maternal and paternal attitudes. *Journal of Family Psychology* **12**(2): 268–88

Bliss (2009) *The Bliss baby charter standards*. Bliss, London

Bliss (2010) *Facts for fathers: Essential advice for fathers of premature or sick babies*. Bliss, London

Bliss (2012) *Bliss baby charter audit tool*. Bliss, London

Brandth B, Kvande E (1998) Masculinity and childcare: the reconstruction of fathering. *The Sociological Review* **46**(2): 293-313

Brannen J, Nilsen A (2006) From fatherhood to fathering: Transmission and change among British fathers in four generation families. *Sociology* **40**(2): 335–52

Bryanton J, Beck CT (2010) Postnatal parental education for optimizing infant general health and parent–infant relationships. *Cochrane Database of Systematic Reviews* Issue 1. Art. No.: CD004068. DOI: 10.1002/14651858.CD004068.pub3.

Burgess A (1997) *Fatherhood reclaimed: The making of the modern father*. Vermillion, London

Burgess A (2007) *The costs and benefits of active fatherhood: Evidence and insights to inform the development of policy and practice*. Fathers Direct, London

Burgess A (2008) *Maternal and infant health in the perinatal period: The fathers' role*. Fatherhood Institute, London

Burkitt I (1997) Social relationships and emotions. *Sociology* **31**(1): 37–55

Button TMM, Maughan B, McGuffin P (2007) The relationship of maternal smoking to psychological problems in the offspring. *Early Human Development* **83**: 727–32

Cabrera NJ, Tamis-LeMonda CS, Bradley RH, Hofferth S, Lamb ME (2000) Fatherhood in the twenty-first century. *Child Development* **71**(1): 127–36

Carter JD, Mulder RT, Darlow BA (2007) Parental stress in the NICU: The influence of personality, psychological, pregnancy and family factors. *Personality and Mental Health* **1**: 40–50

Christiansen SL, Palkovitz R (2001) Why the 'good provider' role still matters: Providing as a form of paternal involvement. *Journal of Family Issues* **22**(1): 84–106

Cone S (2007) The impact of communication and the neonatal intensive care unit environment on parent involvement. *Newborn and Infant Nursing Reviews* **7**(1): 33–8

Connell RW (1987) *Gender and power: Society, the person and sexual politics*. Polity Press, Cambridge

Connell RW (2005) *Masculinities* (2nd edn). Polity Press, London

Datta J, Graham B, Wellings K (2012) The role of fathers in breastfeeding: Decision making and support. *British Journal of Midwifery* **20**(3): 159–67

Deave T, Johnson D (2008) The transition to parenthood: What does it mean for fathers? *Journal of Advanced Nursing* **63**(6): 626–33

Department of Health (2009) *Toolkit for high-quality neonatal services.* Department of Health, London

Department of Health (2010) *Maternity and early years: Making a good start to family life.* Department of Health, London

Dermott E (2003) The intimate father: Defining paternal involvement. *Sociological Research Online* **8**(4). Available from: http://www.socresonline.org.uk/8/4/dermott. html.> (accessed 20 February 2012)

Dermott E (2006) What's parenthood got to do with it? Men's hours of paid work. *British Journal of Sociology* **57**(4): 619–34

Dermott E (2008) *Intimate fatherhood: A sociological analysis.* Routledge, London

Doering LV, Dracup K, Moser D (1999) Comparison of psychosocial adjustment of mothers and fathers of high-risk infants in the neonatal intensive care unit. *Journal of Perinatology* **19**(2): 132–7

Duncombe J, Marsden D (1998) 'Stepford wives' and 'hollow men'? Doing emotion work, doing gender and 'authenticity' in intimate heterosexual relationships. In: Bendelow G, Williams SJ (eds) *Emotions in social life.* Routledge, London

Duncombe J, Marsden D (1999) Love and intimacy: The gender division of emotion and 'emotion work': A neglected aspect of sociological discussion of heterosexual relationships. In: Allan G (ed) *The sociology of the family: A reader.* Blackwell, Oxford

Earle S (2000) Why some women do not breast feed: Bottle feeding and fathers' role. *Midwifery* **16**: 323–30

Easterbrooks MA, Goldberg WA (1984) Toddler development in the family: Impact of father involvement and parenting characteristics. *Child Development* **55**: 740–52

Eggebean DJ, Knoester C (2001) Does fatherhood matter for men? *Journal of Marriage and the Family Issues* **63**: 81–93

Ekbald M, Korkeila J, Parkkola R, Lapinleimu H, and the PIPARI Study Group (2010) Maternal smoking during pregnancy and regional brain volumes in preterm infants. *Journal of Pediatrics* **156**: 185–90

Ellberg L, Högberg U, Lindh V (2010) 'We feel like one, they see us as two': New parents' discontent with postnatal care. *Midwifery* **26**: 463–8

Equal Opportunities Commission (2006) *Twenty-first century dad.* Equal Opportunities Commission, Manchester

Equal Opportunities Commission (2007) *The state of the modern family.* Equal Opportunities Commission, Manchester

Erlandsson K, Christensson K, Fagerberg I (2008) Fathers' lived experiences of getting to know their baby while acting as primary caregivers immediately following birth. *Journal of Perinatal Education* **17**(2): 28–36

Erlandsson K, Dsilna A, Fagerberg I, Christensson K (2007) Skin-to-skin care with the father after cesarian birth and its effect on newborn crying and prefeeding behavior. *Birth* **34**: 105–14

Erlandsson K, Lindgren H (2009) From belonging to belonging through a blessed moment of love for a child – the birth of a child from the fathers' perspective. *Journal of Men's Health* **6**(4): 338–44

Fagan J, Barnett M (2003) The relationship between maternal gatekeeping, paternal competence, mothers' attitudes about the father role, and father involvement. *Journal of Family Issues* **24**(8): 1020–43

Fägerskiöld A (2008) A change in life as experienced by first-time fathers. *Scandinavian Journal of Caring Science* **22**(1): 64–71

Fatherhood Institute (2007) *Including new fathers: A guide for maternity professionals.* Fatherhood Institute, London

Fatherhood Institute (2009) *Fathers and parenting programmes. What works.* Fatherhood Institute, London

Fatherhood Institute (2011) *Annual report 2010–11*: Bringing dads into the picture. Fatherhood Institute, London

Feeley N, Gottlieb L, Zelkowitz P (2007) Mothers and fathers of very low birth weight infants: Similarities and differences in the first year after birth. *Journal of Obstetrics, Gynecological and Neonatal Nursing* **36**: 558–67

Ferketich SL, Mercer RT (1995) Paternal–infant attachment of experienced and inexperienced fathers during infancy. *Nursing Research* **44**(1): 31–7

Ferri E, Smith K (1996) *Parenting in the 1990s.* Family Polices Study Centre & Joseph Rowntree Foundation, London & York

Finn M, Henwood K (2009) Exploring masculinities within men's identificatory imaginings of first-time fatherhood. *British Journal of Social Psychology* **48**: 547–62

Finnbogadöttir H, Crang Svalenius E, Persson EK (2003) Expectant first time fathers' experiences of pregnancy. *Midwifery* **19**(2): 96–10

Flouri E (2005) *Fathering and child outcomes.* J Wiley and Sons, Chichester

Flouri E, Buchanan A (2003) The role of father involvement in children's later mental health. *Journal of Adolescence* **26**(1): 63–78

Flouri E, Buchanan A (2004) Early father's and mother's involvement and child's later educational outcomes. British Journal of Educational Psychology **74**(2): 141–53

Forste R, Bartkowski JP, Allen-Jackson R (2009) 'Just be there for them': Perceptions of fathering among single, low-income men. *Fathering* **7**(1): 49–69

Gagnon AJ, Sandall J (2007) Individual or group antenatal education for childbirth or parenthood, or both. *Cochrane Database of Systematic Reviews* Issue 3. Art. No.: CD002869. DOI: 10.1002/14651858. CD002869.pub2

Goodman JH (2008) Influences of maternal postpartum depression on fathers and on father–infants interaction. *Infant Mental Health Journal* **29**(6): 624–43

Greenhalgh R, Slade P, Spiby H (2000) Fathers' coping style, antenatal preparation, and experiences of labor and the postpartum. *Birth* **27**(3): 177–84

Gregory A, Milner S (2011) What is 'new' about fatherhood? The social constriction of fatherhood in France and the UK. *Men and Masculinities* **14**(5): 588–606

Grossman KE, Grossman K, Zimmermann P (1999) A wider view of attachment and exploration: Stability and change during the years of immaturity. In: Cassidy J, Shaver PR (eds) *Handbook of attachment: Theory, research, and clinical applications*. Guilford Press, New York

Hamilton A, deJonge D (2010) The impact of becoming a father on other roles: An ethnographic study. *Journal of Occupational Science* **17**(1): 40–6

Hearn J (2004) From hegemonic masculinity to the hegemony of men. *Feminist Theory* **5**(1): 49–72

Henderson AD, Brouse AJ (1991) The experiences of new fathers during the first 3 weeks of life. *Journal of Advanced Nursing* **16**(3): 293–8

Henwood K, Procter J (2003) The 'good father': Reading men's accounts of paternal involvement during the transition to first time fatherhood. *British Journal of Social Psychology* **42**(pt3): 337–55

Hildingsson I, Thomas J, Engström-Olofsson R, Nystedt A (2009) Still behind the glass wall? Swedish fathers' satisfaction with postnatal care. *Journal of Obstetric, Gynecological and Neonatal Nursing* **38**: 280–9

Hochschild AR (1979) Emotion work, feeling rules, and social structure. *American Journal of Sociology* **85**(3): 551–75

Hochschild AR (1994) The second shift: Employed women are putting in another day of work at home. In: Kimmel MS, Messner MA (eds) *Men's lives* (3rd edn). Allyn and Bacon, Needham Heights MA

Holditch-Davis D, Bartlett TR, Blackman AL, Miles MS (2003) Post traumatic stress symptoms in mothers of premature infants. *Journal of Gynecological and Neonatal Nursing* **32**(2): 161–71

Howell E, Graham C (2011) *Parents' experiences of neonatal care: A report on the findings from a national survey*. Picker Institute Europe, Oxford

Hugill K (2009) *The experiences and emotion work of fathers in a neonatal unit*. Unpublished PhD thesis. University of Central Lancashire, Preston

Hutchfield K (1999) Family-centred care: A concept analysis. *Journal of Advanced Nursing* **29**(5):1178–87

Jauniaux E, Greenough A (2007) Short and long term outcomes of smoking during pregnancy. *Early Human Development* **83**(11): 697–8

Johnson G, Semmence J (eds) (2006) *Individual Income 1996/97–2004/05*. Women and Equality Unit, National Statistics Office, London

Kaarensen PI, Ronning JA, Ulvund SE, Dahl LB (2006) A randomized controlled trial of the effectiveness of an early-intervention program in reducing parenting stress after preterm birth. *Pediatrics* **118**(1): e9–e19

Kikkert HK, Middleburg KJ, Hadders-Algra M (2010) Maternal anxiety is related to infant neurological condition, paternal anxiety is not. *Early Human Development* **86**: 171–7

Kim HS (2009) Social sharing of emotion words and otherwise. *Emotion Review* **1**(1):

92–3

King M (2011) Stay-at-home dads on the up: One in seven fathers are main childcarers. *The Guardian*. Available from: http://www.guardian.co.uk/uk/2011/oct/25/stay-at-home-dads-fathers-childcarers (accessed 23 January 2012)

Kraemer S (1995) What are fathers for? In: Burck C, Speed B (eds) *Gender, power and relationships*. Routledge, London

Lam J, Spence K, Halliday R (2007) Parents' perception of nursing support in the neonatal intensive care unit (NICU). *Neonatal Paediatric and Child Health Nursing* **10**(3): 19–25

Lamb ME (1998) Fatherhood then and now. In: Booth, A, Crouther AC (eds) *Men in families: When do they get involved? What difference does it make?* Lawrence Erlbaum Associates (LEA), London

LaRosa R (1994) Fatherhood and social change. In: Kimmel MS, Messner MA (eds) *Men's' lives* (3rd edn). Allyn and Bacon, Needham Heights MA

Lawlor DA, Emberson JR, Ebrahim S, et al (2003) Is the association between parity and coronary heart disease due to biological effects of pregnancy or adverse lifestyle risk factors associated with child-rearing? Findings from the British women's heart and health study and the British regional heart study. *Circulation* **107**: 1260–4

Lee T-Y, Miles MS, Holditch-Davis D (2005) Father's support to mothers of medically fragile infants. *Journal of Gynecological and Neonatal Nursing* **35**(1): 46–55

Lemay CA, Cashman SB, Elfenbein DS, Felice ME (2010) A qualitative study of the meaning of fatherhood among young urban fathers. *Public Health Nursing* **27**(3): 221–31

Lindberg B, Axelsson K, Öhrling K (2007) The birth of premature infants: Experiences from the fathers' perspective. *Journal of Neonatal Nursing* **13**(4): 142–9

Lindberg B, Axelsson K, Öhrling K (2008) Adjusting to being a father to an infant born prematurely: Experiences from Swedish fathers. *Scandinavian Journal of Caring Sciences* **22**: 79–85

Locock L, Alexander J (2006) 'Just a bystander'? Men's place in the process of fetal screening and diagnosis. *Social Science and Medicine* **62**: 1349–59

Lundqvist P, Hellström Westas L, Hallström I (2007) From distance toward proximity: Fathers' lived experience of caring for their preterm infants. *Journal of Pediatric Nursing* **22**(6): 490–7

Lundqvist P, Jakobsson L (2003) Swedish men's experiences of becoming fathers to their preterm infants. *Neonatal Network* **22**(6): 25–31

McBride BA, Brown GL, Bost KK, Shin N, Vaughn B, Korth B (2005) Paternal identity, maternal gatekeeping, and father involvement. *Family Relations* **54**: 360–72

McVeigh CA, Baafi M, Williamson M (2002) Functional status after fatherhood: An Australian study. *Journal of Obstetric, Gynaecologic and Neonatal Nursing* **31**(2): 165–71

Magill-Evans J, Harrison MJ, Rempel G, Slater L (2006) Interventions with fathers of young children: Systematic literature review. *Journal of Advanced Nursing* **55**(2): 248–64

Matthey S, Barnett B (1999) Parent–infant classes in the early postpartum period: Need and participation by fathers and mothers. *Infant Mental Health Journal* **20**(3): 278–90

Mezulis AH, Hyde JS, Clark R (2004) Father involvement moderates the effect of maternal depression during a child's infancy on child behavior problems in kindergarten. *Journal of Family Psychology* **18**(4): 575–88

National Childbirth Trust (2012) *Involving fathers: Getting fathers involved.* Available from: http://www.nct.org.uk/professional/diversity-and-access/supporting-dads/ general-resources (accessed 4 April 2012)

National Institute for Health and Clinical Excellence (2006) *Routine postnatal care of women and their babies.* National Institute for Health and Clinical Excellence, London

Obeidat HM, Bond EA, Clark Callister L (2009) The parental experience of having an infant in the newborn intensive care unit. *Journal of Perinatal Education* **18**(3): 23–9

O'Brien M (2005) *Shared caring: Bringing fathers into the frame*, EOC Working Paper Series 18. Equal Opportunities Commission, Manchester

O'Brien M, Shemilt I (2003) *Working fathers: Earning and caring research discussion series.* Equal Opportunities Commission, Manchester

Oommen H, Rantanen A, Kaunonen M, Tarkka M-T, Salonen AH (2011) Social support provided to Finnish mothers and fathers by nursing professionals in a postnatal ward. *Midwifery* **27**: 754–61

Paulson JF, Bazemore SD (2010) Prenatal and postpartum depression in fathers and its association with maternal depression: A meta-analysis. *Journal of the American Medical Association* **303**(19): 1961–9

Pelchat D, Lefebvre H, Levert M-J (2007) Gender differences and similarities in the experience of parenting a child with a health problem: Current state of knowledge. *Journal of Child Health Care* **11**(2): 112–31

Persson EK, Fridlund B, Dykes A-K (2007) Parents' postnatal sense of security (PPSS): Development of the PPSS instrument. *Scandinavian Journal of Caring Sciences* **21**: 118–25

Persson EK, Fridlund B, Kvist LJ (2011) Fathers sense of security during the first postnatal week – a qualitative interview study in Sweden. *Midwifery* doi:10.1016/j. midw.201108.010

Peticuff JH, Arbeart KL (2005) Effectiveness of an intervention to improve parent-professional collaboration in neonatal intensive care. *Journal of Perinatal and Neonatal Nursing* **19**(20): 187–202

Pohlman S (2005) The primacy of work and fathering preterm infants: Findings from an interpretive phenomenological study. *Advances in Neonatal Care* **5**: 204–16

Pontes CM, Alexandrino AC, Osório MM (2008) The participation of fathers in the breastfeeding process: Experiences, knowledge, behaviors and emotions. *Jornal Pediatria (Rio J)* **84**(4): 357–64

POPPY Steering Group (2009) *Family-centred care in neonatal units. A summary of research results and recommendations from the POPPY project.* NCT, London

Premberg A, Hellström A-L, Berg M (2008) Experiences of the first year as father. *Scandinavian Journal of Caring Science* **22**: 56–63

Ramchandani P, Stein A, Evans J, O'Connor TG and the ALSPAC study team (2005) Paternal depression in the postnatal period and child development: A prospective population study. *The Lancet* **365**: 2201–5

Ranson G (2001) Men at work: change–or no change: In the era of the 'new father'. *Men and Masculinities* **4**(3): 3–26

Reeves J, Rehal F (2008) Contextualising the evidence: Young fathers, family and professional support. In: Reeves J (ed) *Inter-professional approaches to young fathers.* M&K Update Ltd, Keswick

Ringland CP (2008) Posttraumatic stress disorder and the NICU graduate mother. *Infant* **4**(1): 14–17

Rowe ML, Cocker D, Pan BA (2004) A comparison of fathers' and mothers' talk to toddlers in low income families. *Social Development* **13**: 278–91

Royal College of Midwives (2012) *Reaching out: Involving fathers in maternity care.* RCN, London

Rustia J, Abbott D (1993) Father involvement in infant care: Two longitudinal studies. *International Journal of Nursing Studies* **30**(6): 467–76

Sarkadi A, Kristiansson R, Oberklaid F, Bremberg S (2008) Fathers' involvement and children's developmental outcomes: A systematic review of longitudinal studies. *Acta Paediatrica* **97**: 153–8

Schoppe-Sullivan SJ, Cannon EA, Brown GL, Mansgelsdorf SC, Szewczyk Sokolowski M (2008) Maternal gatekeeping, coparenting quality, and fathering behaviour in families with infants. *Journal of family Psychology* **22**(3): 389–98

Segal L (1997) *Slow motion: Changing masculinities, changing men* (2nd edn). Virago, London

Seidler VJ (2007) Masculinities, bodies, and emotional life. *Men and Masculinities* **10**(1): 9–21

Sloan K, Rowe J, Jones L (2008) Stress and coping in fathers following the birth of a preterm infant. *Journal of Neonatal Nursing* **14**: 108–15

Smeaton D (2006) *Dads and their babies: A household analysis*, Working Paper Series No. 44. Equal Opportunities Commission, Manchester

Smeaton D, Marsh A (2006) *Maternity and paternity rights and benefits: Survey of parents 2005.* Department of Trade and Industry, London

Spence K, Lau C (2006) Measuring nursing unit culture as an empirical basis for implementing a model of practice in a neonatal intensive care unit. *Journal of Neonatal Nursing* **12**(1): 20–8

Steen M, Downe S, Bamford N, Edozien L (2011) Not-patient and not-visitor: A meta-synthesis of fathers encounters with pregnancy, birth and maternity care. *Midwifery* doi:10.1016/j/midw.2011.06.009

Steinberg S, Kruckman L (2000) Reinventing fatherhood in Japan and Canada. *Social Science and Medicine* **50**(9): 1257–72

Stelle CD, Sheehan NW (2011) Exploring paternal maturity in the relationships between older fathers and adult children. *International Journal of Aging and Human Development* **72**(1): 46–65

St John W, Cameron C, McVeigh C (2004) Meeting the challenges of new fatherhood during the early weeks. *Journal of Obstetrics, Gynecological and Neonatal Nursing* **34**(2): 180–9

Strazdins L, Korda RJ, Lim LL-Y, Broom DH, D'Souza RM (2004) Around the clock: Parent work schedules and children's well-being in a 24-h economy. *Social Science and Medicine* **59**(7): 1517–27

Sullivan O (2000) The division of domestic labour. *Sociology* **34**(3): 437–56

Swallow V, Lambert H, Santacroce S, Macfadyen A (2011) Fathers and mothers developing skills in managing children's long-term medical conditions: How do their qualitative accounts compare? *Child: Care, Health and Development* doi:10.1111/j.1365-2214.2011.01219.x

Sweet L, Darbyshire P (2009) Fathers and breast feeding very-low-birthweight preterm babies. *Midwifery* **25**: 540–53

Tamis-LeMonda CS, Shannon JD, Cabrera NJ, Lamb ME (2004) Fathers and mothers at play with their 2 and 3 year-olds: Contributions to language and cognitive development. *Child Development* **75**(6): 1806–20

Templeton S-K (2011) New dads urged to muck in on maternity ward. *The Sunday Times* 31/11/2011: 7

Theodosius C (2006) Recovering emotion from emotion management. *Sociology* **40**(5): 893–910

Thomas JE, Bonér A-K, Hildingsson I (2011) Fathering in the first few months. *Scandinavian Journal of Caring Sciences* **25**: 499–509

Thompson M, Vinter L, Young V (2005) *Dads and their babies: Leave arrangements in the first year.* EOC Working Paper Series No. 37. Equal Opportunities Commission, Manchester

Tryvaud K, Doyle LW, Lee KJ, Roberts G, et al (2011) Family functioning and parenting stress 2 years after very preterm birth. *Early Human Development* **87**: 427-431

Turan T, Basbakkal Z, Özbck S (2008) Effect of nursing interventions on stressors of parents of premature infants in neonatal intensive care unit. *Journal of Clinical Nursing* **17**(21): 2856–66

Wall G, Arnold S (2007) How involved is involved fathering? An exploration of the contemporary culture of fatherhood. *Gender and Society* **21**(4): 508–27

Warin J, Solomon Y, Lewis C, Langford W (1999) *Fathers, work and family life.* Family

Polices Study Centre & Joseph Rowntree Foundation, London & York

Weiss S, Goldlust E, Vaucher YE (2010) Improving parent satisfaction: An intervention to increase neonatal parent-provider communication. *Journal of Perinatology* **30**: 425–30

White G (2007) You cope by breaking down in private. Fathers and PTSD following childbirth. *British Journal of Midwifery* **15**(1): 39–45

Williams RA (2007) Masculinities fathering and health: The experiences of African-Caribbean and white working class fathers. *Social Science and Medicine* **64**(2): 339–49

Williams S (2008) What is fatherhood? Searching for the reflexive father. *Sociology* **42**: 487–502

Wilson S, Durbin CE (2010) Effects of paternal depression on fathers' parenting behaviours: A meta-analytic review. *Clinical Psychology Review* **30**: 167–80

Wöckel A, Schafer E, Beggel A, Abou-Dakn M (2007) Getting ready for birth: Impending fatherhood. *British Journal of Midwifery* **15**(6): 344–8

Woollett A, Nicolson P (1998) The social construction of motherhood and fatherhood. In: Niven CA, Walker A (eds) *Current issues in infancy and parenthood 3.* Butterworth Heinemann, Oxford

Yaxley D, Vinter L, Young V (2005) *Dads and their babies: The mothers' perspective.* EOC Working paper series 41. Equal Opportunities Commission, Manchester

Zelkowitz P, Papageorgiou A, Bardin C, Wang T (2009) Persistent maternal anxiety affects the interaction between mothers and their very low birthweight children at 24 months. *Early Human Development* **85**(1): 51–8

Chapter 6

Fathers, midwifery and neonatal practice

Kevin Hugill and Merryl Harvey

Introduction

Midwifery and neonatal nursing involves providing care for increasingly diverse families in which fathers are taking a more active role. The starting point for this book was a desire to provide a readily accessible compendium of the literature pertaining to fatherhood and examine how fathers experience fatherhood in midwifery and neonatal contexts. We believe it is important to be aware of this literature and these experiences for a number of reasons. Firstly, developing an increased appreciation of fatherhood from a variety of points of view will equip midwives and neonatal nurses to provide more responsive and inclusive care to fathers, mothers and their children. Secondly, this improved understanding will enable more systematic engagement with fathers at a deeper level, facilitating service review and revision to better meet the needs, expectations and aspirations of fathers and mothers.

This chapter aims to provide an overview of the previous chapters by posing and answering key questions about fatherhood in relation to midwifery and neonatal practice. These questions include consideration of why healthcare professionals should engage with fathers, what influences fathers' behaviours and how midwives and neonatal nurses can facilitate greater involvement of fathers and better meet their needs in practice. Finally we look to the future and pose some potentially fruitful areas for research and consider how to optimise fathers' participation in this research.

Understanding fatherhood

Being a father has important effects on men's status in society and their self-esteem (Eggebean and Knoester, 2001). Whilst over the life course there are positive effects on men's health and wellbeing from being a father, in the early days and years fatherhood can cause significant detriment to men's health and wellbeing (Bartlett, 2004; Foster, 2004). Becoming a father provides opportunities for men to develop their self-confidence, express their emotions and demonstrate their commitment to their family. However, the father role in the early 21st century cannot be considered to be a collective masculine identity. Considerable variation exists in how individuals define what fatherhood involves and how men should behave as fathers. However, for many in the UK, fatherhood can be characterised by its durability and flexibility. This is particularly evidenced in the way in which older ideas have been reinterpreted into current explanations about how fathers should conduct themselves, especially in relation to increased expectations that they will be involved in childcare and family life. Despite the rhetoric, a recent study suggests that fathers only spend around half the time (32.4 minutes for every 60) that mothers spend in caring for and educating their children (Fatherhood Institute, 2010).

Everyone has a picture of who fathers are and what they do, as a result the imagery and language of fatherhood is ubiquitous and can be used to convey many meanings beyond those that this book is concerned with. Because of everyone's widespread pre-understanding, it is important to take account of this in any dealings concerning fathers. Fatherhood has many facets (Connell, 1987) and is simultaneously an individual and a social experience; it is important to understand the effects of these various aspects on individual fathers' behaviours. Gender identity is one aspect that has significant effects on how individuals view the world (Morgan, 1992). It is known that, for men, their ideas about masculine gender identity are highly influential on how they behave in general and as fathers (Smiler, 2004; Vuori, 2009). For example, some men see childcare as unmanly, whilst others hold the opposite view; the basis for these points of view is often deeply embedded in culturally defined norms of acceptable masculine behaviour. However, gender and masculinity are not the only sources of influence, and others, such as interpersonal relationships, political ideology and socioeconomic factors are known to be important. The law with regard to fatherhood is constantly evolving and whilst it to some extent seeks to tackle gender inequalities in parenthood it also seeks to reinforce a father's obligations, particularly financial, towards his children. Legislation also has important implications for healthcare professionals, particularly when seeking consent for a baby's treatment in the early days after birth where the parents are unmarried and the birth not registered. Healthcare professionals need to remain vigilant of the law whilst also taking care not to imply fathers' lesser status, which could add to their feelings of marginalisation.

In general, maternity and neonatal care settings vary in their inclusion of fathers and this affects their experiences and satisfaction with the attention and support they receive (Hildingsson et al, 2009; Harvey, 2010; Oommen et al, 2011; Persson et al, 2011; Steen et al, 2011). In neonatal units, wide variations in parental experience continue to feature in surveys (POPPY Steering Group, 2009; Howell and Graham,

2011). The challenge is to deal systematically with these shortcomings whilst retaining space for innovation. Compared to fathers in more usual circumstances, those whose baby is admitted to a neonatal unit are exposed to additional sources of stress and emotional turmoil. While there are differences, many of these accounts of emotional stress share similarities with those reported from studies with mothers. However, similarities between mothers' and fathers' experiences must be treated with some caution. Just because they are using similar words and phrases to describe their experiences and emotions does not necessarily imply similarity in their appraisals of the causes of those emotions, nor do they place similar regard on their relevance. One of the causes of dissimilarity of experience might be due to differences in the way men and women experience maternity, since women are more biologically and socially embedded in maternity care systems as a consequence of being pregnant. Men, after all, only have contact with maternity care services by virtue of their partner's status and consequently experience it vicariously. A more inclusive and wider reproductive health and pre-parenthood preparation strategy that seeks out, for example, adolescent boys and young men, many of whom will become future fathers, could begin to address this.

Following preterm birth, fathers' emotional responses are influenced by a complex interplay between their own perceptions and what they and others think is appropriate (Hugill, 2009). Fathers seem to benefit from opportunities to share their worries but at the same time there is a need to recognise many men's desire to present a façade of inner control. Research has shown that men often expect and are expected by others to be emotionally stronger to support their partner (Hugill, 2009; Harvey, 2010). This behaviour could be problematic in neonatal units and possibly in other adverse situations around childbirth. For example, some fathers edit information they perceive as potentially upsetting when speaking to their partner. However, the effects of this censorship on mothers' experiences is unknown and other, less protective, interpretations are possible; this behaviour might reflect some men's desire to express their power or regain some control. Healthcare professionals need to be cognisant of this behaviour when using fathers as intermediaries to communicate with mothers or other family members. It is unclear, but such behaviours might have implications for men's wellbeing and health.

Why engage with fathers?

Existing political and professional policy and legislation in the UK requires health, education and social services and those working in them to take responsibility for improving children's wellbeing. They are also responsible for addressing any gender inequalities in their services and the ways they deliver them. Together, this means that engaging with fathers and families to encourage fathers' greater involvement should feature in all organisations that have contact with them. Another way to look at this is that including fathers is not optional, and healthcare professionals should seek out ways and opportunities to ensure their practice is more father inclusive. As a consequence, fathers are no longer peripheral to the business of maternity and neonatal care. When we were researching fathers' experiences it was clear to us that many healthcare professionals were aware of fathers and their needs and adapted their practice in order to be inclusive. Unfortunately, such awareness and accommodation is not universal (Hildingsson et al, 2009; Steen et al, 2011). Currently, the UK lags behind similar comparator nations (ranked 18th out of 21) on a series of indicators relating to aspects of men and women's public and private lives (Fatherhood Institute, 2010). This suggests there is scope for further improvement in relation to gender equality and family friendly practices and policies.

Law, political policy and practice are constantly changing and each informs the other; in relation to fatherhood this relationship is particularly pertinent and fast moving. Healthcare professionals need to remain acquainted with current knowledge and understanding of best practice. The current UK policy context sees encouragement of greater paternal involvement, and preparation for and commitment to family life as imperative. However, whilst many advocate for this, it is not an easy change for many areas of healthcare, and numerous difficult obstacles remain. On one level, these barriers relate to theoretical and philosophical concerns, such as different understandings of what involvement means and the effects of fathers' choices/ intentions and mothers' attitudes. Others include more pragmatic concerns, such as family economic circumstances and men's long working hours, for example. Overarching these concerns there is evidence that the ways in which health, social and educational services are organised continue to perpetuate assumptions that mothers are, or should be, the primary care providers within the family. This situation will limit or exclude fathers' access to potential sources of information and support.

The challenge for those working in midwifery and neonatal care settings is twofold: firstly to challenge residual pockets of resistance to father engagement amongst some men and women and healthcare professionals, and secondly to move beyond philosophical endorsement of father involvement and ensure that it is universally implemented. Strategic leaders, managers, service commissioners, healthcare professionals, mothers and fathers need to work together to develop credible services that support the achievement of this ambition for greater father involvement and bring about the benefits for all that this entails.

From the outset, fathers are highly influential in women's pregnancy and childbirth choices. While in the past fathers were less obviously involved in their children's everyday life, they have always been influential on the health and wellbeing of their children, although not always positively. More recently, reinterpretations of father roles and academic modelling of fathers' behaviours now see fathers as more directly involved in childcare and family life (Masciadrelli et al, 2006). Research in recent decades concerning the effects of greater father involvement in different contexts and across international boundaries consistently reiterates the many positive effects of fathers' involvement on mothers', children's and fathers' lives (Allen et al, 2007; Burgess, 2007). Given the existing legislative and policy framework and the enormity of the potential benefit to mothers, their children and society in general from addressing fathers' needs and expectations, the arguments for incorporating fathers into everyday midwifery and neonatal practice are compelling.

What influences fathers' levels of involvement?

Fatherhood demonstrably entails a number of cultural contradictions in that fathers are encouraged to become more active in childcare and family life and yet simultaneously expected to provide economically for their family, whether this economic provision is voluntary or enforced through legislative structures, such as the courts or Child Support Agency. This inconsistency remains culturally relevant for modern-day British fathers and most report issues with reconciling the various tensions that emerge from this position. Despite this situation, many men see the work they do as an important aspect of their masculine identity (Hearn, 1992; Morgan, 1992; Collinson and Hearn, 1996; Burghes et al, 1997), and following fatherhood it can become an increasingly important way for them to express their commitment to and involvement in family life, both in usual and more complicated circumstances (Pohlman, 2005; Allen et al, 2007; Hugill, 2009).

Fathers are not alone in experiencing significant economic and social changes; during similar timeframes, women's lives as mothers and in general have also undergone significant upheaval. In recent years, work patterns for men and women have changed, although economic cycles seem to affect men and women differently (Warin et al, 1999; Equal Opportunities Commission, 2006, 2007). Women now make up 75% of the part-time workforce (Fatherhood Institute, 2010) and this suggests some enduring gender inequality in balancing work and family life. This situation might help to explain why mothers contribute more childcare even when both parents work (Hochschild, 1994; Sullivan, 2000) but does not explain whether this is by choice or circumstance.

Becoming a father is one of the many transitions that men make during their lives, and having a child generally increases men's connectivity with others. Some fathers see this process as more significant than other life changes. Perhaps this is because of its multifaceted nature and the way fatherhood touches upon all aspects of men's lives. Despite its importance, few fathers feel fully prepared for the impact that becoming a father has on their lives and many subsequently feel that it is a challenging process (Buist et al, 2003; Genesoni and Tallandini, 2009; Chin et al, 2011). During the time of transition, fathers seek to make emotional connections with their child and begin to renegotiate existing relationships; many men are uncertain as they do not know how to act or what is expected of them. Healthcare professionals can help fathers by involving them in antenatal preparations and postnatal support by recognising that this period of transition is not a straightforward process, even when not complicated by factors such as youth and mental illness, or adverse events, such as preterm birth.

A significant source of influence on fathers is mothers (Yaxley et al, 2005). Mothers' attitudes affect and shape fathers' involvement in childcare through processes referred to as 'maternal gatekeeping' (Allen and Hawkins, 1999; McBride et al, 2005; Schoppe-Sullivan et al, 2008). However, fathers' own behaviours and attitudes also play an important part in facilitating or confounding their access to and reception from healthcare professionals. In responding to this, midwives and neonatal nurses can limit, control or mediate fathers' involvement. The actions and attitudes of staff can inadvertently reinforce dated stereotypical expectations about how fathers should normally behave, thus compounding fathers' feelings of marginalisation and exclusion.

How can healthcare professionals support fathers and facilitate greater involvement?

Healthcare professionals who seek to support fathers participate in a complex endeavour in that they are attempting to influence the culture of fatherhood and fathers' behaviours whilst at the same time trying to keep in mind that fathers are individuals with unique needs and desires. Most fathers in the UK attend the birth and immediate care of their baby (Kiernan and Smith, 2003; TNS System Three, 2005). This can include normal, complicated and preterm deliveries and situations when the baby requires resuscitation at birth. Whether all fathers wish to do this is debatable. For fathers who attend the birth of their baby their status has over time moved on from merely witnessing events towards one that includes significant elements of participation in proceedings. Despite this, fathers report experiencing a range of positive and negative emotions and say that they are unclear of their role and receive limited support from healthcare professionals before, during or after the birth to perform their expected roles (White, 2007; Castle et al, 2008; Kunjappy-Clifton, 2008). This can be particularly acute and problematic for fathers who witness the resuscitation of their baby (Harvey, 2010, 2012). At times, for fathers, confusion about their status and responsibilities in midwifery and neonatal settings can be an additional source of stress. This situation can arise when healthcare professionals view and prioritise things differently from fathers and fail to communicate this. In general, despite some innovative practice ideas and developments (Fatherhood Institute, 2007; Royal College of Midwives, 2012), the needs of fathers are often not adequately considered in the configuration and provision of maternity and neonatal services.

In addition to equipping themselves with the skills to communicate effectively with fathers, and setting time aside to offer support, nurses and midwives can act on fathers' behalf by advocating for facilities for them, such as a place where they can rest or reflect in private. Furthermore, providing continuity of carer throughout pregnancy, birth and the postnatal period or through a neonatal unit stay is known to positively affect mothers' and fathers' experiences of support and satisfaction; lobbying for adequate staffing resources so that services can be configured to ensure this, would seem to be worthwhile. Arguably, as fathers have become more concerned with providing childcare, the boundaries between motherhood and fatherhood have become blurred. This situation provokes questions about whose interest this development serves; what the consequences for mothers, fathers and their children are; and how fathering is differentiated from mothering.

Evidence to date suggests that there are subtle differences between how mothers and fathers provide and perceive childcare and this might have an important bearing on children's socialisation. Many first-time fathers either aspire to be like their own father or conversely do things differently. This attitude reflects the highly influential role past experiences of being fathered have on determining men's fathering style and how they wish to father.

Fatherhood in a neonatal unit can present fathers with a unique set of additional challenges and opportunities. Competing fatherhood agendas and the difficult emotional circumstances they find themselves in can result in fathers feeling pulled in many conflicting directions at the same time. Fathers in general seem unable to synthesise all these demands and this provides an additional source of stress. However, it is important to view these difficulties in perspective as ultimately, most seem to cope, and for some men even normal childbirth can precipitate a personal crisis. Healthcare professionals can help fathers to recognise these tensions, can explain uncertainties and that it is normal sometimes to feel powerless and overwhelmed, and can also assist them to set achievable goals.

The early postnatal period provides an ideal opportunity for healthcare professionals to engage with fathers, particularly as many fathers are both available and receptive during this time. There are some promising initiatives and policy developments that are begining to capitalise on the opportunities this time offers to engage with fathers, to equip them with relevant skills and to promote greater involvement. Unfortunately, it is an opportunity that is seldom used to its full advantage. Because of the way postnatal care is delivered, there are some major cultural and social obstacles that continue to prevent fathers from becoming fully included in family services that have historically been aimed at mothers. While most now accept that including fathers is in general a good thing, debates about the relative merits of including fathers in the early postnatal period, both in maternity and neonatal care, and in particular how best to achieve the benefits from this inclusion, are ongoing.

Teaching parents about their baby can be helpful in sensitising them to their baby's behaviour and needs (Appleton, 2011). There is some evidence that such knowledge can promote improved baby outcomes, particularly for preterm babies (Kaarensen et al, 2006; Westrup, 2007). When these activities are incorporated into a structured programme this might promote more positive parenting behaviours and general parenting efficacy. Programmes aimed at reducing mothers' stress experiences by developing their coping strategies can be helpful (Feeley et al, 2011), however evidence of any similar effect on fathers' stress is uncertain. This might be because the cause of stress in fathers differs from that in mothers, or that the programmes used in studies lack gender sensitivity.

Broadly speaking, there is still insufficient research into which sort of interventions are best for increasing engagement with and supporting fathers to establish their roles. However, in more difficult or problematic circumstances, interventions which seek to challenge fathers' assumptions and behaviours or increase their emotional coping strategies and resilience seem to be beneficial (Magill-Evans et al, 2006; Fatherhood Institute, 2009). However, the evidence as to whether generic or bespoke, single or mixed gender, small groups or one-to-one programmes are best at helping to inform and support fathers is ambiguous. There are probably many reasons for this, including the effects of self-selecting participants, the programme provider's father-inclusive behaviours (or lack of), and the nature and content of programme materials. Notwithstanding these limitations, experience suggests that when fathers are provided with opportunities they view as timely, accessible and meaningful to their concerns then they readily agree to take part.

Child caring experience of fathers is variable; there is an assumption, not always borne out, that second or multiple-time fathers are more equipped than first-time fathers. Fathers, like mothers, need to develop their childcare skills in the postnatal period, and services need to be structured in a way that offers them opportunities to do this. Rather than relying upon fathers accessing existing forums during antenatal and postnatal periods, there is a need to evaluate and review the content, timings and settings of existing provision to ascertain whether or not they are 'father friendly'. There is some merit in reaching out to new and prospective fathers by focusing upon direct interventions with them and seeking out new and innovative places and ways to engage with them. In this respect, much could be gained from adapting some of the strategies used in projects that aim to broaden men's engagement around their health needs (see also Conrad and White, 2007; White and Witty, 2009).

Men's decisions about father involvement and their fatherhood identity are influenced by their own, their partners' and other family members' experiences of pregnancy, childcare and family life. In order to foster greater engagement with fathers it is important to reconsider their roles and contributions beyond that limited to participation in childcare activities alone. Importantly, research suggests that mothers and fathers want fathers to be viewed as individuals who are striving to meet the needs of their family and who are important contributors to decision-making; but the challenge to move from visitor to legitimate participant remains. Fathers can be acutely aware of or fearfully anticipate discriminatory attitudes towards them, and healthcare professionals should be mindful to avoid rushing to make judgements about their abilities and suitability, which might not be accurate. Healthcare professionals can also help to make fathers feel more welcome and increase their visibility in their practice areas, for example, by auditing their environment for father friendliness, seeking out additional opportunities to involve them, speaking with fathers and making them aware of the importance of their contributions, and in particular developing an awareness of the powerful emotional and behavioural effects that their own non-verbal communication can have upon fathers and what they infer is and is not 'allowed'.

Modern ideas about fathers and fatherhood contain elements that are both contiguous with past generations and simultaneously at odds with them (Pleck,

1997; Brannen and Nilsen, 2006). These ideas are framed by reference to gender politics, intimate relationships, the law and governmental policy, and men's past experiences, aspirations and expectations. Fatherhood now features widely in academic literature and the popular media. However, some views of fatherhood either reinforce existing stereotypes or present innovative gender relationships as somewhat out of the ordinary. Consequently, despite increasing attention to the subject, fatherhood remains rather nebulous, leaving us with the widespread notion that everyone knows what we are talking about and referring to but its exactness remains reassuringly elusive.

Looking to the future

In this book we have mainly focused on maternity and early infancy. However, we are conscious that this does not reveal a complete picture of fatherhood identity, roles and relationships. In part this reflects the intentions of this book but also reflects the dearth of attention given to the longitudinal study of fatherhood throughout the life course. Fatherhood is a lifelong role and goes beyond the spheres of midwifery and neonatal practice, and in order to develop a fuller understanding of fatherhood there is a need for more research concerning fathers' relationships with their older children in usual and more complicated contexts; this includes father relationships with their adult children who might be parents themselves. Equally, many aspects of fatherhood are undergoing a period of profound social change, and contemporary understandings of fatherhood must be viewed in light of these developments and emerging trends; cross-generational studies could draw attention to the nature and impacts of these changes on men's, women's and their children's lives.

Research about fathers

Many fathers, when asked, talk about everyday clashes between 'being men' and 'being in families' (O'Brien and Shemilt, 2003; Vuori, 2009). This might be because of discord between the lived realities of men and women and existing social constructs of gender roles. Some suggest that instead this conflict has arisen because family relationship studies have tended to focus upon mothers' viewpoints and have as a result become 'feminised' (Morgan, 2001) or 'domesticated' (Francis, 2002). To address this, Marsiglio and colleagues, writing at the beginning of the 21st century (Marsiglio et al, 2000), called for a greater emphasis on first-hand accounts from men themselves. More recent research literature suggests that this ambition has been partly achieved. However, considerable gaps remain and what we know about fathers' lives remains fairly limited.

Over recent years, the study of fatherhood has developed its own distinctive agendas in many differing fields, including healthcare, psychology and sociology. Men's experiences as fathers are coming to the fore in research, and increasing attempts to include men are apparent. A number of questions have emerged whilst preparing this book that require further thought and empirical study. Future research could take a number of interesting directions, but it is clear that practically every area of fatherhood research to date would benefit from more development and additional study. This could include extending our understanding into different groups of fathers, additional aspects of fatherhood experience, such as the interplay between gender and emotion, or the effects of political policy on fathers' everyday lives. We also need to develop a more detailed understanding of service effectiveness in relation to fathers. This could be done by carrying out evaluations of existing and innovative midwifery and neonatal interventions and processes in terms of multiple outcomes, such as, mothers, children, families, wider societal effects and service efficacy. There is also a need for more extensive research into most areas of fathers' postnatal and neonatal experiences to determine their expectations and needs during this time.

There are a number of additional questions that researchers could develop that might be appropriate to maximise future understanding of fatherhood in midwifery and neonatal contexts. Whilst the following list of sample questions is not intended to be exhaustive, it does demonstrate the scope of opportunities available to potential researchers:

- What is the relationship between different varieties of fathering style and what influences individual men to adopt a particular style in preference to another?
- How do fathers integrate academic models of fatherhood into their ideas about fathering?
- How do fathers model their fathering behaviour and what are the sources and relative importance of these influences?
- How do fathers' ideas about fatherhood evolve over the life course?
- How effective are particular strategies in promoting father involvement and what contextual factors affect their success?
- How does fathers' presence during events around complicated and normal childbirth affect mothers' birth experiences and the behaviours of healthcare professionals?

- How do fathers articulate their emotional distress when witnessing distressing events in normative and non-normative ways?
- What are the long-term effects on fathers from been present during adverse childbirth events and how can we provide specific support during and after these events?
- What sort of antenatal and postnatal preparations for fatherhood should we provide both in relation to fatherhood in general and in neonatal units?
- What are the most effective strategies to use when working with fathers in difficult circumstances and with challenging behaviours?
- What can healthcare professionals do to support fathers to enable them to better manage their status as information and communication intermediaries?

Research with fathers

Engaging and involving fathers in research can present researchers with practical and logistical challenges (Macfadyen et al, 2011). However, these difficulties are not insurmountable. In our experience, many fathers engage readily with research, if and when they are given the opportunity to do so (Hugill, 2009; Harvey, 2010). Nevertheless, researchers may encounter hurdles to be overcome when they try to involve fathers in their studies. Fathers are generally less accessible to researchers and this means they can be difficult to recruit. In the past, this inaccessibility was largely because limited information was documented about a child's father, particularly if the parents were not married. The work patterns of some fathers can also mean they are difficult to access, and maternity and early childhood services are often still almost exclusively mother-focused (Jackson, 1983; Lewis and O'Brien, 1987; Macfadyen et al, 2011). The long-standing focus on mothers in parenting research has also led many fathers to assume that their feelings, experiences and points of view are unimportant (Harvey, 2010, 2012; Macfadyen et al, 2011).

Sometimes fathers may be reluctant to participate in research because they do not want to disclose their experiences and feelings in the presence of their partner. This may be for a number of reasons; they may not want to distress her, they may be aware that they have contrasting views, or they may feel they should not appear to be weak or vulnerable (Lupton, 1998; Harvey, 2010; Macfadyen et al, 2011). Sometimes, particularly in the home environment, their partners may be acting as gatekeepers preventing researchers from accessing them (Mackereth and Milner, 2009). In contrast Korotchikova et al (2010) report more instances of parents agreeing to participate in research when they are asked together. For some men it might be that social sharing of inner emotional states with those beyond immediate intimate circles can imply an undesired familiarity (Hugill, 2009; Kim, 2009). Some fathers may feel uncomfortable at the prospect of sharing their thoughts and feelings with a female researcher, particularly if they feel the research topic to be a sensitive issue (Walls et al, 2010; Macfadyen et al, 2011). Indeed, when given the opportunity, many welcome the chance to talk to male researchers (Arockiasamy et al, 2007; Hugill, 2009), although female researchers have found that this discomfort is not universal, as fathers are also willing to talk to them (Clark and Miles, 1999; Fägerskiöld, 2008; Harvey, 2010). Clearly, whilst interpretations of gender relationships and men's emotional world views offer some explanation of men's reluctance to participate in research, they are overly simplistic, and more complex explanations are required. Finally, some groups of fathers can be particularly difficult to access and recruit, such as young fathers and fathers who are living in violent or impoverished communities (Foster, 2004). However, the researcher should not be deterred.

There are a number of strategies that researchers can utilise that may be appropriate to maximise the involvement of fathers in parenting research:

- Involving fathers in the development and design of research proposals and participant information documentation.
- Seeking collaboration with or endorsement by service user groups that are known to support fathers or high-profile male role-models.
- Making themselves available 'out of hours', i.e. in the evenings, at weekends and on public holidays, to recruit fathers.
- Endeavouring to recruit fathers in a direct way rather than via their partner.
- Offering a range of venues for data collection. These may include the father's home or place of work.
- Providing opportunities for data collection to take place 'out of hours', i.e. in the evenings, at weekends and on public holidays.
- Providing opportunities for fathers to participate in data collection separately from their partner.
- Having the option of a male or female researcher to undertake participant recruitment and data collection.
- Offering a range of data collection methods, including online format.
- Offering incentives for participation.
- Using snowball sampling methods.
- Offering to provide participants with a summary of the study's findings.

(After: Foster, 2004; Macfadyen et al, 2011; Involve, 2012)

Final thoughts

It is difficult to explain the nature and meanings of fatherhood dispassionately; fatherhood tends to arouse deep emotions and in part this is because it connects with people's personal experiences. It is about more than natural biological events and a particular set of behaviours; it is multifaceted, involving a dynamic and diverse socio-culturally mediated performance. Evidence suggests that complex and ongoing social processes are continuing to operate, the influence of which requires men to renegotiate their fatherhood roles. Contemporary fatherhood is not a stable concept; it exists within a malleable framework of rights and responsibilities and it is a phenomenon around which there are competing discourses. Consequently, our understanding of fatherhood remains rather opaque, but it seems to represent an amalgamation of idealised traditional roles with emerging, and at times contradictory, role expectations in which greater gender equality in childcare and family life are coming to the fore.

Fatherhood cannot be condensed into a single category of experience and role and it is more than a curtailed version of motherhood; it exists in a plurality of forms. It might be that incorporating increased attention to negotiation with fathers early on about what they want to do, rather than making assumptions that getting 'hands-on' is best for all men, might negate some of the negativity some fathers experience from healthcare professionals. Ways to achieve this in practice should be explored. A key premise running through this book emphasises the emotionality of fatherhood and the sometimes tense relationship between individuals' deeply ingrained ideas and attitudes about fathers and what it is they do in contrast to newer emerging typologies of fathering. Stemming from this tension, there are two key messages that midwives, neonatal nurses and other healthcare professionals can take from this book. The first is that having an awareness of their own attitudes about fathers and how this affects their interactions with them is vital. Second, if in doubt about how to engage with fathers, the best and most simple strategy is to be open and honest and just talk with them on an emotional level, asking about their hopes, aspirations and uncertainties.

Reflective activity
Over to you

Throughout this book we have concluded each chapter with case histories based upon real-life situations and events that provide an opportunity for readers to reflect on these cases and relate them to their practice experiences. We believe that the separation of individuals' private and professional lives is somewhat artificial and that each affects the other. Negating the relationships between these autobiographical threads can contribute to stress, emotional dissonance and poor performance. In this final chapter we hope that you will construct your own case history and using what you have learnt from this book reflect upon your own experiences of fatherhood and how these have influenced your beliefs about fathers and attitudes towards them, both in everyday life and practice. This activity will enable readers to acknowledge the sources of their well-established beliefs and also support fathers more effectively, regardless of their own beliefs.

Constructing your case history

Thinking back to your own childhood and early adult life what are your recollections of being fathered? Include things that are both positive and less positive and other influences on family life.

Reflective questions

- Did and does your appraisal of what was good and bad change over time?
- If you have siblings do their recollections have similarities with yours or are there significant differences and why do you think this might be so?
- To what extent did your experiences of fatherhood reflect the norms of the time when you were a child?
- In light of your past experiences how would you want your children to be fathered?
- How do you define a good father, what are the key qualities?
- In relation to your field of practice, are fathers important and valued and why?
- Consider what arrangements are in place in your place of work to support fathers, do these work and how can they be improved?

References

Allen S, Daly K with Father Involvement Research Alliance (2007) *The effects of father involvement: An updated research summary of the evidence.* Centre for Families, Work and Well-Being, Guelph ON

Allen SM, Hawkins AJ (1999) Maternal gatekeeping: Mothers' beliefs and behaviours that inhibit greater father involvement in family work. *Journal of Marriage and the Family* **61**(1): 199–212

Appleton J (2011) Newborn behavioural aspects. In: Lomax A (ed) *Examination of the newborn.* Wiley Blackwell, Chichester

Arockiasamy V, Holsti L, Albersheim S (2007) Fathers' experiences in the neonatal intensive care unit: A search for control. *Pediatrics* **121**(2): e215–22

Bartlett EE (2004) The effects of fatherhood on the health of men: A review of the literature. *Journal of Men's Health and Gender* 1(2–3): 159–69

Brannen J, Nilsen A (2006) From fatherhood to fathering: Transmission and change among British fathers in four generation families. *Sociology* **40**(2): 335–52

Burgess A (2007) *The costs and benefits of active fatherhood: Evidence and insights to inform the development of policy and practice.* Fatherhood Institute, London

Burghes L, Clarke L, Cronin N (1997) *Fathers and fatherhood in Britain.* Family Policy Study Centre, London

Buist A, Morse CA, Durkin S (2003) Men's adjustment to fatherhood: Implications for obstetric health care. *Journal of Obstetric, Gynecologic and Neonatal Nursing* **32**: 172–80

Castle H, Slade P, Barranco-Wadlow M, Rogers M (2008) Attitudes to emotional expression, social support and postnatal adjustment in new parents. *Journal of Reproductive and Infant Psychology* **26**: 195–210

Chin R, Hall P, Daiches A (2011) Fathers' experiences of their transition to fatherhood: A metasynthesis. *Journal of Reproductive and Infant Psychology* **29**(1): 4–18

Clark SM, Miles MS (1999) Conflicting responses: The experiences of fathers of infants diagnosed with severe congenital heart disease. *Journal of the Society of Pediatric Nurses* **4**(1): 7–14

Collinson D, Hearn J (1996) 'Men' at 'work': Multiple masculinities/multiple workplaces. In: Mac An Ghaill M (ed) *Understanding masculinities: Social relations and cultural arenas.* Open University Press, Buckingham

Connell RW (1987) *Gender and power: Society, the person and sexual politics.* Polity Press, Cambridge

Conrad D, White AK (2007) *Men's health: How to do it.* Radcliffe Publishing, Oxford

Eggebean DJ, Knoester C (2001) Does fatherhood matter for men? *Journal of Marriage and the Family Issues* **63**: 81–93

Fägerskiöld A (2008) A change in life as experienced by first-time fathers. *Scandinavian Journal of Caring Science* **22**(1): 64–71

Equal Opportunities Commission (2006) *Twenty-first century dad.* Equal Opportunities Commission, Manchester

Equal Opportunities Commission (2007) *The state of the modern family.* Equal Opportunities Commission, Manchester

Fatherhood Institute (2007) *Including new fathers: A guide for maternity professionals.* Fatherhood Institute, London

Fatherhood Institute (2009) *Fathers and parenting programmes. What works.* Fatherhood Institute, London

Fatherhood Institute (2010) *The Fatherhood Report 2010–11. The Fairness in Families Index.* Fatherhood Institute, London

Feeley N, Zelkowitz P, Westreich R, Dunkley D (2011) The evidence base for the Cues program for mothers of very low birth weight infants: An innovative approach to reduce anxiety and support sensitive interaction. *Journal of Perinatal Education* **20**(3): 142–53

Foster J (2004) Fatherhood and the meaning of children: An ethnographic study among Puerto Rican partners of adolescent mothers. *Journal of Midwifery and Women's Health* **49**(2): 118–25

Francis M (2002) The domestication of the male? Recent research on nineteenth and twentieth-century British masculinity. *The Historical Journal* **45**(3): 637–52

Genesoni L, Tallandini MA (2009) Men's psychological transition to fatherhood: Analysis of the literature, 1989–2008. *Birth* **36**(4): 305–17

Harvey ME (2010) *The experiences and perceptions of fathers attending the birth and immediate care of their baby.* Unpublished PhD Thesis. Aston University, Birmingham

Harvey ME (2012) Being there: A qualitative interview study with fathers present during the resuscitation of their baby at delivery. *Archives of Disease in Childhood Fetal and Neonatal Edition* doi:10.1136/archdischild-2011-301482

Hearn J (1992) *Men in the public eye: The construction and deconstruction of public men and public patriarchies.* Routledge, London

Hildingsson I, Thomas J, Engström-Olofsson R, Nystedt A (2009) Still behind the glass wall? Swedish fathers' satisfaction with postnatal care. *Journal of Obstetric, Gynecological and Neonatal Nursing* **38**: 280–9

Hochschild AR (1994) The second shift: Employed women are putting in another day of work at home. In: Kimmel MS, Messner MA (eds) *Men's lives* (3rd edn). Allyn and Bacon, Needham Heights MA

Howell E, Graham C (2011) *Parents' experiences of neonatal care: A report on the findings from a national survey.* Picker Institute Europe, Oxford

Hugill K (2009) *The experiences and emotion work of fathers in a neonatal unit.* Unpublished PhD Thesis. University of Central Lancashire, Preston

Involve (2012) Available from: http://www.involve.org.uk/

Jackson B (1983) *Fatherhood.* George Allen & Unwin, London

Kaarensen PI, Rønning JA, Ulvund SE, Dahl LB (2006) A randomized controlled trial of the effectiveness of an early-intervention program in reducing parenting stress after preterm birth. *Pediatrics* **118**: e9–19

Kiernan K, Smith K (2003) Unmarried parenthood: New insights from the Millennium Cohort Study. *Office for National Statistics Population Trends* **Winter**: 114.

Kim HS (2009) Social sharing of emotion words and otherwise. *Emotion Review* **1**(1): 92–3.

Korotchikova I, Boylan GB, Dempsey EM, Ryan CA (2010) Presence of both parents during consent process in non-therapeutic neonatal research increases positive response. *Acta Paediatrica* **99**: 1484–8

Kunjappy-Clifton A (2008) And father came too…. a study exploring the role of first time fathers during the birth process and to explore the meaning of the experience for these men: Part two. *MIDIRS Midwifery Digest* **18**: 57–66

Lewis C, O'Brien M (1987) What good are dads? *Father Facts* **1**(1): 1–12

Lupton D (1998) *The emotional self.* Sage Publications, London

McBride BA, Brown GL, Bost KK, Shin N, Vaughn B, Korth B (2005) Paternal identity, maternal gatekeeping, and father involvement. *Family Relations* **54**: 360–72

Macfadyen A, Swallow V, Santacroce S, Lambert H (2011) Involving fathers in research. *Journal for Specialists in Pediatric Nursing* **16**: 216–19

Mackereth C, Milner SJ (2009) 'He'll not talk to anyone': Researching men on low incomes. *Community Practitioner* **82**(4): 24–7

Magill-Evans J, Harrison MJ, Rempel G, Slater L (2006) Interventions with fathers of young children: Systematic literature review. *Journal of Advanced Nursing* **55**(2): 248–64

Marsiglio W, Amato P, Day RD, Lamb ME (2000) Scholarship on fatherhood in the 1990s and beyond. *Journal of Marriage and the Family* **62**(4): 1173–91

Masciadrelli BP, Pleck JH, Stueve JL (2006) Fathers' role model perceptions. *Men and Masculinities* **9**(23): 23–34

Morgan DHJ (1992) Discovering men. Routledge, London

Morgan DHJ (2001) Families, gender and masculinities. In: Whitehead SM, Barrett FJ (eds) *The masculinities reader.* Polity Press, Cambridge

O'Brien M, Shemilt I (2003) *Working fathers: Earning and caring research discussion series.* Equal Opportunities Commission, Manchester

Oommen H, Rantanen A, Kaunonen M, Tarkka M-T, Salonen AH (2011) Social support provided to Finnish mothers and fathers by nursing professionals in a postnatal ward. *Midwifery* **27**: 754–61

Persson EK, Fridlund B, Kvist LJ (2011) Fathers' sense of security during the first post-natal week – A qualitative interview study in Sweden. *Midwifery* doi:10.1016/j.midw.201108.010

Pleck JH (1997) Paternal involvement: Levels, sources and consequences. In: Lamb ME (ed) *The role of the father in child development* (3rd edn). Wiley, New York NY

Pohlman S (2005) The primacy of work and fathering preterm infants: Findings from an interpretive phenomenological study. *Advances in Neonatal Care* **5**: 204–16

POPPY Steering Group (2009) *Family-centred care in neonatal units. A summary of research results and recommendations from the POPPY project.* NCT, London

Royal College of Midwives (2012) *Reaching out: Involving fathers in maternity care.* Royal College of Nursing, London

Schoppe-Sullivan SJ, Cannon EA, Brown GL, Mansgelsdorf SC, Szewczyk Sokolowski M (2008) Maternal gatekeeping, coparenting quality, and fathering behaviour in families with infants. *Journal of Family Psychology* **22**(3): 389–98

Seidler VJ (1997) *Man enough: Embodying masculinities.* Sage, London

Smiler AP (2004) Thirty years after the discovery of gender: Psychological concepts and measures of masculinity. *Sex Roles: A Journal of Research* **50**(1–2): 15–26

Steen M, Downe S, Bamford N, Edozien L (2011) Not-patient and not-visitor: A meta-synthesis of fathers' encounters with pregnancy, birth and maternity care. *Midwifery* doi:10.1016/j.midw.2011.06.009

Sullivan O (2000) The division of domestic labour. *Sociology* **34**(3): 437–56

TNS System Three (2005) *NHS maternity services quantitative research.* TNS System Three, Edinburgh

Vuori J (2009) Men's choices and masculine duties: Fathers in expert discussions. *Men and Masculinities* **12**(1): 45–72

Walls P, Parahoo K, Fleming P, McCaughan E (2010) Issues and considerations when researching sensitive issues with men: Examples from a study of men and sexual health. *Nurse Researcher* **18**(1): 26–34

Warin J, Solomon Y, Lewis C, Langford W (1999) *Fathers, work and family life.* Family Polices Study Centre & Joseph Rowntree Foundation, London & York

Westrup B (2007) Newborn Individualized Developmental Care and Assessment Program (NIDCAP): Family-centered developmentally supportive care. *Early Human Development* **83**: 443–9

White A, Witty K (2009) Men's under use of health services. Finding alternative approaches. *Journal of Men's Health* **6**(2): 95–7

White G (2007) You cope by breaking down in private: Fathers and PTSD following childbirth. *British Journal of Midwifery* **15**: 39–45

Yaxley D, Vinter L, Young V (2005) *Dads and their babies: The mothers' perspective.* EOC Working paper series 41. Equal Opportunities Commission, Manchester

Index